ENDORSEMENTS

Count to One is a passionate and majestic call to contend for Christian unity. As one who has prayed, dreamed and hoped for a miraculous and tangible breakthrough in unity across the historic streams of our faith, I confess this book is unlike any I have read. If your heart cries and your eyes weep for the coming together of the Body of Christ, you must join Bishop Robert on his amazing journey of revelation. "Together. Unstoppable. One Body."

Dr. Jeff Farmer, President
Pentecostal/Charismatic Churches of North America

I have known and worked with Bishop Robert on some of the most sensitive international issues that I have engaged as Chief Counsel of the American Center for Law & Justice. His timely and important call for unity is the right message at this critical juncture. *Count to One* is a must read.

Jay Sekulow
American Center for Law and Justice, Chief Counsel

"Behold how good and how pleasant it is for brothers to dwell together in unity."

This well-preached and often-sung verse holds the key to a release of the power of God's Spirit that few have experienced because it is so seldom practiced! In this, his first published work, Bishop Robert re-examines the critical events and times that separated believers and robbed the Church of her intended authority and power. This message taps into the truth of the gospel and holds the key to worldwide revival when millions will be swept into the Kingdom of God in a great last days demonstration of the power of the one true Living God; "for there the Lord commands His blessing, even life forevermore."

Paul Wilbur
Integrity Music Artist and Award-Winning Author of
Touching the Heart of God
www.WilburMinistries.com

Written in the true spirit of Oneness! Bishop Robert captures the heart and the goal of where the Church with a Capital "C" is being led in these last days as a Bride preparing herself through the working of the Holy Spirit for the glorious wedding feast with her Bridegroom, Jesus.

Bishop Robert has written a clear understanding of the Bride's pathway and journey. He has also disentangled the web of misunderstanding so that we clearly see the goal in sight.

This amazing book is not just full of valuable information, it is also extremely practical and set for the body of Christ's use in this critical "hour." It is challenging, comforting, and healing to the soul. It is exactly what our great Physician has ordered to bind up our brokenness in the Body.

Bruno Ierullo, Senior Pastor
Catch The Fire Newmarket (Toronto Airport Fellowship)

Bishop Robert has a deep love for God and for the people of God, and an unwavering faith in the purposes to which the Church has been called.

In *Count to One*, Bishop Robert challenges us as brothers and sisters—a family in faith—to examine our common and collective identity in Christ. Our society—both nationally and globally—is tremendously fragmented and fractured. In a fashion that is compelling, scripturally-grounded, and well-reasoned, he reminds us of the directive we have received from our Father God to stand on the common ground, that is the gospel, and to function together in a way that is cohesive, complementary, and mutually edifying. Only when we live out the unity we were created for, can we powerfully fulfill God's calling on each of us, and the mission He has for the Church.

Count to One is a timely and powerful exhortation for the Church in our time.

Reverend Luis Cortés, Jr.
President/CEO of Esperanza

Down through the pages of history whenever Christ followers have expressed their faith in unity they have powerfully impacted their world. *Count to One* reminds us that we are able to release the power of God as we live, work and pray in unity. Living in a world that is plagued with conflict, fear and disharmony we have a unique opportunity to start a 'unity' revolution with our brothers and sisters in Christ from every racial, cultural, economic, political and denominational background. As we stand together we can practically live out the gospel of Jesus displaying His love to a lost and hurting world. Now is a time to use our diversity as a platform for unity and to show the world that we are His disciples as we truly love one another. (John 13:35)

Graham Power
Founder of Global Day of Prayer & Unashamedly Ethical

We are indeed grateful to our brother in Christ, Bishop Robert Gosselin, for his inspiring and practical book which calls all Christians to begin and end with the One, who alone is the Alpha and Omega, our Lord and Savior Jesus Christ. I had the unique joy of working with Bishop Robert as the Orthodox and Catholic Churches worked in harmony to prepare for the historic prayer service in the Holy Sepulcher and meetings between His Holiness Pope Francis and His All Holiness Ecumenical Patriarch Bartholomew in Jerusalem.

Bishop Robert worked on that historic pilgrimage because of his desire to see all Christian brothers and sisters dwelling in unity as the One Body of Christ. *Count To One* helps brings that impossible dream of Ecumenical Oneness into a realm of spiritual possibility which can be both appreciated and comprehended.

As Ecumenical Patriarch Bartholomew admonishes, "we must converse as Christians among ourselves to resolve our differences so that our witness to the outside world may be credible. It is not possible for the Lord to agonize over the unity of His disciples and for us to remain indifferent about the unity of all Christians. That would constitute criminal betrayal and transgression of His divine commandment."

Bishop Robert's testimony in *Count to One* assures that he will not be numbered as one of the transgressors of our Lord's divine commandment "that we all may be one".

Fr. Alex Karloustos
Protopresbyter of the Ecumenical Patriarch
Greek Orthodox Archdiocese of America
New York, NY

Bishop Robert's personal journey among several of the streams of historic Christianity provides a template for understanding his compelling call for followers of Jesus to discover the spiritual reality of the "One" stream of faith that undergirds all of God's work in Christ. Flowing into these different streams are the tributaries, small and large, in which most of us find ourselves organizationally connected. But in these latter days, it is imperative we discover that our unity in Christ transcends our limited perspectives. The Holy Spirit is inviting all of us to join the great journey described in this important book. You will find this book an engaging and insightful read.

Dr. A.D. Beacham, Jr.
General Superintendent and Presiding Bishop
The International Pentecostal Holiness Church
Oklahoma City, Oklahoma USA

The modern movement for Christian unity has taken a major leap forward through the relationship of charismatic Anglican Bishop Tony Palmer and Pope Francis. Their deep friendship in Christ launched a surprisingly new and vibrant path for Catholics and evangelical Protestants to travel together. In this context Bishop Robert, who comes from the same ecclesial fellowship as Tony Palmer, presents a heartfelt plea for doing whatever it takes to build Christian unity. As a charismatic Catholic who shares this desire, I was delighted to read this book, to rejoice in our shared convictions, to ponder afresh some of our differences, and to pray with the text for deeper understanding of today's leadings of the Holy Spirit.

For a writer who claims to be neither a theologian nor a historian, he does an admirable job in both areas, combining erudition with much testimony and folksy reminiscences. I find controversial issues presented in such a way as to invite further brotherly discussion rather than controversy. So, for example, I would look forward to conversation about his evangelical teaching on the new birth and my Catholic understanding of baptismal regeneration. Or when he says that the Church is relational and not institutional, I would like to hit the pause button and suggest that this is a matter of both/and rather than either/or. After all, serious ecumenism requires serious discussion.

I want to point out several sections of the book which I find outstanding. First, Bishop Robert makes an impassioned plea for Eucharistic fellowship across ecclesial divides. His presentation will, I think, move many Catholic charismatics. We pray for the day when our own Church will be led by the Spirit towards such sweet communion. Second, his affirmation of the tenets of the Nicene Creed as a foundation for building unity is very helpful. Third, his chapter on God's glory, his own glory, his glory in and among us and through us into the world is very, very good. It should be read several times. It is an opportunity to stop and pray, both to contemplate and to open oneself to the glory of God and to understand in a growing way its relationship to genuine love and therefore to real unity. Finally, Bishop Robert gives us a section on forgiveness that is both deeply moving and challenging. Here one senses that the most difficult wrongdoing can be brought to the grace of forgiveness. Seemingly insurmountable incidents of hurt can be healed in Christ. Forgiveness, genuinely sought and granted, restores brotherhood and enables unity in the one Body of Christ.

Count to One is both a refreshing encouragement and a valuable tool in the work of building Christian unity.

Deacon Kevin M. Ranaghan, Ph.D.
People of Praise, Founder

Table of Contents

Before We Begin: The Groundwork 11

Chapter 1: Reflections on Christian Unity 19

Chapter 2: "I Hear There are Divisions Among You" 35

Chapter 3: Discerning the Body 47

Chapter 4: In Christ 71

Chapter 5: Historical Foundations 87

Chapter 6: Unity—Not Uniformity 101

Chapter 7: Unity—Not Unification 115

Chapter 8: For the Sake of the Glory 123

Chapter 9: Dealing with the Differences 135

Chapter 10: A Path Forward 155

Epilogue: Dealing with Discipline 173

Questions for Individual Study and Reflection 183

Questions for Group Study and Reflection 195

How Can I Be Sure I Know Jesus? 203

About the Author 209

Before We Begin: The Groundwork

Sometimes I hate reading God's Word!

Not always, of course. The fact is that I usually truly enjoy the time I spend studying the Bible. But sometimes what He has to say to me is simply far too convicting or challenging.

Now I know that, for many Christians, reading the Bible is an important part of their daily routine. Some believers prefer a fairly unstructured approach, choosing to read pretty much whatever comes to mind on that particular morning or evening. Others take a more structured approach, using some sort of a daily devotional or even Scripture readings set out in the *Book of Common Prayer*. There are any number of choices in between.

As I said, there are lots of times when I really do enjoy spending quiet mornings with the God of the Word and take great strength, wisdom, and encouragement from His Word. I tend to be fairly structured and read through the New Testament from beginning to end on a regular basis, adding selected readings from the Old Testament throughout the year and the occasional topical study. So maybe "hate" is an overly strong word choice, because I usually love reading the Bible.

Usually, that is.

But there are times when God allows my determination to spend time in His Word to become a dry and difficult chore. Times when He challenges me to persevere until I break through to a new level of intimacy. For me (and every other Christian who has gone through times like this), walking in the Scriptures closely resembles a marriage relationship. As any married person will admit, if they are honest, maneuvering through the ebb and rise of the emotional elements of a marriage can be a tricky thing. Marriages are not all roses and sunshine. But pressing through the tough times to new depths of love and commitment is rewarding beyond measure. It is the dark times that make us appreciate the light all the more, developing a depth of relationship that holds inestimable value.

Dry times in a marriage are difficult enough, but dry times with the Creator of the universe can be absolutely overwhelming. And then, there are times when the Word of God is just plain convicting. Mornings when it seems as though God is sticking a bony finger in our chest and poking, forcing us to deal with something.

A few years ago, after battling through one of those dry times, I was reading through the New Testament. The Lord arrested me in Ephesians, chapter 4. I use the term *arrested* because, day after day, regardless of my planned reading program, I found myself returning to the same chapter and re-reading those same words. Even when I would decide that I had spent enough time in Ephesians 4 and deliberately started to study a different book or began a specific topical study, the Lord's conviction would come upon me and give me no peace until I turned back to what had, by now, become a very familiar passage.

This continued on for several months. Finally, I decided to directly ask the Lord what He was doing. I am not one who frequently speaks of receiving a message from God. I am very careful before I declare that He has said a specific thing prophetically or directly, because I don't want to be guilty of putting words into His mouth. But in this instance, His answer was clear, direct, and frankly, a bit unsettling. He simply said,

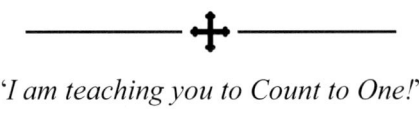

"I am teaching you to Count to One!"

I'll be the first to confess that my mathematics skills are not the stuff that legends are made of. In fact, my feeble attempts to do all but the simplest math in my head are sort of a running joke in my family.

Thankfully, the Lord wasn't really talking about math. He was talking about unity. The light of understanding dawned as the words of Ephesians 4:4-6 flooded my mind.

> There is *one* body and *one* Spirit—just as you were called to *one* hope when you were called—*one* Lord, *one* faith, *one* baptism; *one* God and Father of all, Who is over all and through all and in all. (Emphasis added)

The Lord's determination to see the unity of His Body restored, and His desire to see the power of His glory displayed to a lost and dying world struck me with deliberate force. He desires to see His Body as one—a powerful and life-changing reflection of His own ministry on Earth. But His Church has degenerated into a relatively powerless conglomeration of over 33,000 different (and frequently exclusive) denominations.

ONE!
One Body.
One Spirit.
One Hope.
One Lord.
One Faith.
One Baptism.
ONE GOD.

If there is only ONE GOD (and there is), and if there is only ONE BODY (and according to Him, there is), then perhaps we need to examine why we are so divided. Especially when it is so clearly the will of God that we be united.

It is precisely this examination of unity that I want to explore with you. I happen to believe that the division which pervades the Body of Christ is disgraceful. We are those who are commanded in no uncertain terms by Our Lord to be united, yet we choose to remain apart. I'm afraid if we listen carefully, we may hear Him asking, "Why do you call me, 'Lord, Lord,' and don't do the things which I say?"[1]

Let's hit the "surprising" element head-on, shall we? As you read, you'll note that in several of the chapters of this book, I pay a good deal of attention to the actions of Pope Francis and his efforts to reach out to his brothers and sisters in Christ from other Christian faith expressions. This is a fact that I know will likely be of significant concern to many. Allow me to explain my reasoning and then to ask a favor of you as the reader.

The reason I must give such focus to Pope Francis is that, for the first time in most of our memories, we find the chair of the Bishop of Rome filled by a man who claims to be a born-again, Spirit-filled, and charismatic believer in Jesus Christ. Though I was raised a Roman Catholic, at the age of twenty-one I had a personal encounter with Jesus Christ in an Assemblies of God congregation in Kailua Hawaii. As a result, I felt compelled to leave the Roman Catholic Church. To be frank, I had become convinced there was no reason to remain. I thought the Catholic Church and their doctrines were spiritually dead. So one can imagine the immense level of personal difficulty with which I began to examine this topic anew.

Initially, I had not the slightest interest in considering a "convergence" of what I saw as dead liturgy with my Spirit-filled worship. I was solidly evangelical, thoroughly charismatic and enjoying it! I saw no need to muck-it-up, thank you very much! It took a period of years, and some consistent prodding from a man I see as one of my fathers in the faith, before I began to understand the lessons the Lord was trying to teach me. In chapter five, we'll examine the major lessons I had to learn in more detail. For now, I'll just share two kernels of truth which the Lord opened my eyes to see.

The first kernel was that I *was* liturgical, even though I didn't know it. The charismatic, pentecostal church I worshipped in had its own liturgy; we just didn't call it that. Each and every service began with a pastoral prayer. This was followed by the worship team leading the congregation in three, four, or five songs. At that point, the pastor would come to the platform and pray for specific needs, often sharing words of knowledge about particular maladies in the congregation. More often than not, there would be a word in

---
[1] Luke 6:46

tongues and then, an interpretation (typically by the same two individuals). Then we would have a time of greeting one another, after which a sermon would be delivered. The final element would always be an altar call, first for salvation and then for rededication or a response to the message. This is a liturgy, to be sure, in pretty much every sense of the word.

The second kernel of truth I learned came out of the first. I came to understand that there was no such thing as "dead liturgy," only liturgy being performed by individuals who were either spiritually alive or spiritually dull and dead. It was either the abundance or lack of spiritual life and power in the leaders and participants which opened or closed the door to the presence and impact of the Holy Spirit in the worship service, not the liturgy itself. This is even true in congregations that would never describe themselves as charismatic or pentecostal.

I discovered that liturgy formed the sides of the vessel into which God would pour His Spirit. Within the order of the liturgy, people could worship with incredible freedom. I also came to see the value of many of the historical elements of liturgical worship, especially the way in which these elements were able to draw congregants into greater personal participation in worship.

Learning these lessons forced me to begin considering the convergence of the sacramental, the evangelical, and the charismatic. It brought me to a place where I found myself compelled to return to significant elements of my spiritual roots. To re-examine the baby I had almost thrown out with the bath water. (Truth be told, in some ways I had thrown out the baby and kept the bath water.) This re-examination, of course, required me to consider my roots in the Roman Catholic Church, its position on salvation, and its present leader. (I deal with this in significant detail in chapter four.) I confess that I was amazed to discover some noteworthy foundational developments here. This is not a journey I have completed, nor do I claim to have ascertained all (or even most) of the answers.

The favor I ask of you is this:

Let's take an exploratory journey together. As much as you are able, approach and examine the information I provide to you with an open mind. Some of the "old wineskins" we are holding onto are not well suited to hold the new wine of what the Lord is doing in these days. Read the Scripture references I provide. Study for yourself the points I assert, pray for the wisdom we are promised in James 1:5, and let the Lord guide your mind and your heart.

The first church was as diverse as we are today. Yet they were able to overlook several elements of difference in its members and work as one to proclaim the message of the gospel. Perhaps we can recapture the spirit of grace and understanding that allowed them to preach the gospel *together*. In an amazingly short period of time, they turned the world upside down with the good news. They had no Internet, no cell phones, no jets, and no cars. Imagine what a unified Body of Christ could accomplish today!

There is an unmistakable move of God occurring across the world today. It holds the seeds of promise for the restoration of renewed unity and power in the Body of Christ. THE Body of Christ,—in all of its elements— eyes, ears, arms, legs, noses and 'toeses' all working together as ONE BODY to accomplish the task for which we were created. That unity will be the answer to the prayer of Jesus recorded in John 17 and will lead to manifestations of His glorious power to a lost and dying world.

In this book, I intend to explore what the Lord is doing today in His Church, and propose some solid steps we can *all* take to move closer to the unity that Jesus prayed for in John 17.

Perhaps I haven't learned to *Count to One* yet, but I am working on it with fervent determination.

If you have looked at the Church and wondered whatever happened to the power displayed in the book of Acts…

If you have read the Scriptures and asked yourself if there is a way to return to the ministry of power depicted there…

If your heart has yearned to experience the unity of the Spirit through the bond of peace about which Paul spoke[2]…

…then read on!

Let's see if we can learn to *Count to One*, shall we? Together.

---

[2] Ephesians 4:3

WARNING! I USE BAD LANGUAGE IN THIS BOOK

One more thing before we begin. Let me give you a word of fair warning: I use "bad language" throughout this book.

First of all, I absolutely refuse to capitalize the word *satan*. I understand the rules of grammar as they relate to proper nouns, but I am simply stubborn on this point.

Secondly, I insist on capitalizing the "C" when I am referring to the Church, meaning specifically those persons who have placed their faith in Jesus Christ as the basis for their salvation. I do the same referring to the Body of Christ, capitalizing the "B." This is to clearly differentiate the Church that is the *entire* Body of Christ from any specific church or denomination that is a single element of it. My goal in doing this is to draw the attention of the reader to the intrinsic unity in the Church Christ intended to establish.

The other element of bad language is this; it is cumbersome to continually write "he/she," and its various counterparts when referring to people in the abstract. Yes, I know that using the plural "they" when referring to a singular individual is incorrect and unacceptable. (I know this because it is one of my most common grammatical pitfalls and one for which I receive correction all too often.) So, as a matter of convenience, I have taken the "he" route. I do not imply (or believe) that only men are involved in either the pursuit or leadership of Christian unity, nor that church division is strictly a male issue. There are plenty of both blame and accolades to share between the genders. It just happens to be easier to use one simple pronoun. And, for this, I ask your indulgence.

Chapter 1

REFLECTIONS ON CHRISTIAN UNITY

I spend upwards of 220 days a year traveling, and I have worked on projects on five continents in the past few years. Everywhere I travel, I run into believers to whom the Lord is speaking about unity among Christians. They speak of the Lord leading them into a heart of unity with other believers. Often, they are drawn by the amazing impact of the first century church, in spite of the opposition it faced. They have a desire to return to the place of power in which the seminal generation of Christians stood. Whether millennial or Gen Xer, under thirty or senior—all want to impact their generation.

In short, they want to turn the world upside down again.

What fascinates me is the way in which this unity is being discussed. Because, without exception, everyone with whom I have spoken says the same thing. It is UNITY AMONG CHRISTIANS—not among Christian denominations—which is being spoken of with such longing.

It is as though believers fear our institutions and denominations may have become too entrenched in their ways. (This may be why our efforts at denominational unity routinely fall short of the mark.) Believers seem intrinsically aware that denominations may have great difficulty being able to reach outside of the walls they have built up for themselves. It is as if the traditions they have stood upon have hardened like concrete around their feet.

But the fetters binding our organizations have not stopped the yearning for unity among the believers in those organizations. They have not quenched the desire of the Church—the *true* Church comprised of all those who name Christ as their Lord—to be rejoined as one body.

Paradoxically, and perhaps even more striking, is that this desire is being expressed by leaders at the highest levels of some of the largest Christian entities, in spite of the reservations of some others in their denominations. It's a conundrum and an amazing move of God.

Pentecost 2015 found close to four thousand pentecostal evangelical Christians from around the world gathered in Jerusalem for an event that was billed as a global congress. I was there as large delegations came from almost every continent on Earth, with the largest groups coming from Asia—mainly from Indonesia and China. Africa, Europe, and the Americas were also well represented. Key among the stated objectives of the event was to witness a greater convergence and collaboration of Spirit-empowered ministries around the world in order to unite the global Spirit-filled community together inter-generationally. These objectives were seen as critical to accomplishing the vision that, by the year 2033 (which will be the 2000th anniversary of Jesus' ascent into heaven), every person on the planet will have had an opportunity to respond to the gospel of Jesus Christ. It was an amazing and extraordinarily powerful experience. God was definitely on the move.

It was awe-inspiring to be in the arena as songs of worship to Jesus Christ began to burst forth from the gathered masses. Here were people from divergent regions of the earth, dozens of different denominations, and who knows how many different cultures, and we were all worshipping Jesus Christ in His power and majesty. It was like a brief glimpse of the scene John reveals for us in the book of Revelation, Christ's followers gathered before His throne, crying out: "Holy, Holy, Holy" with all of their heart.

I remember sitting in one of the executive suites, which ring the upper level of the Pais Arena in Jerusalem, where the events were held. It was being used by a global Christian television network to do interviews and air their programming for the event. As I sat there looking out over the thousands and thousands of people filling the arena, it was all I could do to hold back the tears. I found myself asking, "Why can't this be the norm for the Body of Christ? Why can't we celebrate our love for Jesus in the midst of our differences?"

Everyone who had come to Jerusalem had come with the intent to gather together and glorify the name of Jesus. We were focused on Him and what He had done. We were gathered to glorify Him, to lift up His name, and exalt His magnificent beauty. We weren't concerned with which version of the Bible a person had brought with him. No one was standing at the doors asking if we were pedo-baptist or credo-baptist. There weren't separate lines for people who spoke in tongues and for those who did not, nor for Arminians and Calvinists. No special doors existed for those who accepted the doctrine of original sin versus those who held to prevenient grace. We were just a group of people who had been saved by receiving Jesus as our Lord and Savior. And so, we wanted to get together and demonstrate our love for Him.

> Why can't we celebrate our love for Jesus in the midst of our differences?

In doing that we also laid aside our differences and demonstrated our love for one another. Knowing Jesus and loving Him was a sufficient basis for us to gather together and praise Him. One evening I saw several elderly leaders from a broad range of denominational backgrounds being honored for their lifetime of service to the King of Kings. As their names were called and their stories told, everyone stood and applauded. Everyone gave honor to these Kingdom warriors who had invested their lives in proclaiming the gospel of the King. It made no difference if the observers were part of the specific denomination of the leader being honored. We were "just Christians," giving honor where honor was due.

On those nights, in that arena in Jerusalem, there was unity. And the Almighty was glorified. Greatly!

The question still hangs in the air. Why can't it be that way from day to day, church to church, among every person who claims the name of Jesus? *Why not?*

Let's now swing from one edge of the Christian universe to the other, shall we?

Bartholomew is the 270th Archbishop of Constantinople. His position places him as "first among equals" in the leadership of the Orthodox Church, which is comprised of some six-hundred million Orthodox, Coptic, and auto-cephalic (self-ruling) believers in various churches and synods. It is the second largest Christian entity in the world. For almost two decades, Patriarch Bartholomew has been a voice for unity among Christians. He has been deliberate about reaching out to his brothers and sisters in Christ, encouraging dialogue. In 2013, in a startling break with a thousand years of tradition, he boldly accepted an invitation from Jorge Mario Bergoglio to attend the Roman Catholic mass that would install him as Pope Francis.

To fully appreciate the significance of this move, we need to run the clock back to the year 1054. Up until that point the Church had essentially been *one entity* located in many places. There had been several arguments and they had faced numerous issues, even heresies, to be sure. Questions about when and how Jews should be accepted into congregations, rules about what was and wasn't acceptable in a worship service, and arguments about baptism, circumcision, and diet had been more-or-less addressed by various church-wide ecumenical councils, the first of which we read about in Acts 15.

That is not to say that everyone was totally pleased with every decision of these councils or even that there were not serious issues remaining. Unresolved issues remained between Jewish believers and Gentile believers, and their disagreements were particularly thorny. The Church argued as it struggled to make sense of the different natures of Jesus. But internal disagreements and political positioning notwithstanding, Christ's Body was essentially still the "one, holy, catholic and apostolic Church."[3]

All that changed in 1054, in a move that has come to be known as the Great Schism of the Church. For it was in that year the one Church made the decision to split itself into two very separate entities. The decision was an acrimonious one, and each of the two "true" churches blamed the other for the split, issued anathemas (curses) against the other side and among other things, refused to welcome one another at the Lord's Table. This sad state of affairs has continued pretty much unabated until the present day.

---

[3] The term "catholic" means "universal," and relates to the Church that is planted all over the world. It is not exclusively a term related to the Roman Catholic Church. The word was intended to describe the foundational beliefs of a united Church spread across the globe.

In mid-1963, Athenagoras was the Ecumenical Patriarch and Paul VI was the Pope. They initiated a dialogue aimed at beginning to break down the walls that had separated the two leading elements of the Christian Church for most of a millennium. In January of 1964 they met in Jerusalem at the Church of the Holy Sepulcher, embraced as brothers, and rescinded the curses of excommunication which had separated Eastern and Western Christianity for over nine hundred years. Though this was far from a complete restoration of communion, it was a highly significant step.

Fast-forward about five decades to the days of Ecumenical Patriarch Bartholomew, and we find Cardinal Bergoglio leading the Roman Catholics of Argentina. Determined to be a bridge builder, Bergoglio was seeking to establish a dialogue that would restore broken relationships. When he was selected as Pope, Bergoglio took the decision to reach out to Bartholomew, a man he knew possessed a similar desire for restoration. Hence the invitation that placed both Bartholomew and Francis in St. Peter's Square on that historic day in March of 2013. It was the first time the Patriarch of Constantinople had attended the installation of the Bishop of Rome in over one thousand years! For Francis' part, he had deliberately invited Bartholomew to broaden the bridge over the great divide. Driven by a deep desire to see Christians reunited as one body, the new Pope was determined to take a bold step towards establishing a closer relationship. It was a step Bartholomew intended to build upon, as well.

In honor of his esteemed guest, Pope Francis instructed that a section of the installation liturgy, which had historically been read in Latin, be read in Greek. Bartholomew recognized the significance of this act and decided to reciprocate. He devised a plan to advance the dialogue his predecessor had begun some fifty years earlier. After Francis had been installed as Pope, he and Bartholomew had a private meeting. The new Pope was presented with an historic invitation.

"Francis, my brother," Bartholomew began, "Next year will mark the fiftieth year since our predecessors Athenagoras and Paul met in Jerusalem. Let's you and I meet there to advance what they began, shall we?"

Francis accepted without hesitation, leading to the historic meeting in Jerusalem in May of 2014, between Pope Francis and Patriarch

Bartholomew—who, incidentally, oversee the two largest Christian communions in the world![4] Not only did this meeting represent a meaningful and noteworthy reunion of the leaders of the two largest bodies in Christendom, but it was yet another significant step towards restoration of full communion.

It was an amazing event to see, one in which I had the privilege of participating. The various meetings between these two leaders were highly symbolic and extraordinarily momentous; especially our gathering for a joint prayer service at the Church of the Holy Sepulcher. This was the same church where Athenagoras and Paul had met fifty years before. Naturally, their endeavor was not without its critics or its controversy. I'll address the fears and claims of the detractors of this important meeting a bit further on in this chapter and even more so in the next one. But first, let's take a look at another example.

I turn your attention now to a voice for unity, breaking out in two very distinct segments of Christianity—between Evangelicals and Roman Catholics—in order to discuss a ground-shaking breakthrough, orchestrated by my friend the late Bishop Tony Palmer. This story occurred in January 2014 at the Kenneth Copeland Ministers Conference in Fort Worth, Texas.

Bishop Tony came to Christ as a young man in South Africa. Immediately afterwards, he and his wife Emiliana felt compelled to share the gospel with every family living in their sub-division. So, over the next eighteen months, they systematically went door-to-door, telling each of their 3,500 neighbors about Jesus. "Before we used to go out in the morning to do this evangelization, door-knocking," Bishop Tony recalled, "we used to watch this crazy Texan preach the gospel—a guy named Kenneth Copeland. He used to be our encourager every morning." Palmer would eventually begin working for KCM South Africa, and Copeland became one of the first people to support Palmer's ministry. Copeland regularly invited Bishop Tony to attend his annual KCM Ministers Conference as his guest.

At this point, they had been friends for over twenty years, and Tony

---

[4] According to the Pew Research Center, Christians number 2.2 billion, or about one-in-three (32%) people worldwide. About half of all Christians are Catholic (50%). An estimated 37% of Christians belong to a Protestant tradition. The Orthodox Communion, including the Greek and Russian Orthodox, make up 12% of Christians, or about 264 million in the Orthodox communion, making it the second largest, single Christian denomination behind the Catholic Church.

had come to esteem Kenneth Copeland as one of his spiritual fathers. The several previous events of their long friendship notwithstanding, the 2014 conference was going to be unlike any other, and even Brother Copeland called attention to it. As he was introducing Bishop Tony he announced to those in attendance, "You're going to talk about tonight for a long time!" He paused for a moment and then repeated himself to underscore the importance of his announcement. "I said, 'You're going to talk about tonight for a LONG TIME!'"[5] Truer words have seldom been spoken.

Most of those in attendance were likely quite surprised to find a bishop from the Communion of Evangelical Episcopal Churches,[6] simply clad in a black clergy shirt, addressing them that day. Copeland's introduction, as well as his warm personal welcome as Tony came to the platform, made it clear that Kenneth Copeland loved and accepted Tony Palmer. But no one sitting in that Fort Worth auditorium could have anticipated the unprecedented call for unity that was about to be delivered by this young, unassuming cleric.

As he had been asked to do by Brother Copeland, Bishop Tony began by giving some background on his long-standing connection to Copeland, his personal story, and especially the message he had come to deliver. In what I would consider to be a strong candidate for the "Understatement of the Year" award, Tony described it as something "really, really special and historic."

After describing how he and his wife had come to know about KCM, Bishop Tony went on to describe how he had become friends with the Roman Catholic bishop in Argentina. Never one to stand on titles or formality, Archbishop Bergoglio had refused to let his friend address him by any of the styles normally associated with the Roman episcopacy; insisting on being called simply "Father Mario." A born-again, Spirit-filled believer in Jesus Christ, Mario Bergoglio was a true man of faith with a heart for simplicity and a deep desire for unity to be restored to the Body of Christ. Fr. Mario would endear himself to Tony and become another spiritual father to him as the years passed. He would also become the Bishop of Rome,

---

[5] Search YouTube for *"The Miracle of Unity has Begun: KCM Minister's Conference 2014"* to view Bishop Tony Palmer's entire presentation to the 2014 KCM Minister's Conference.

[6] The CEEC is a convergence communion of believers in Jesus Christ who embrace all three streams of historic Christianity: the sacramental, the evangelical and the charismatic. See www.ceecweb.org for more information.

change his name to "Francis," and assume leadership of the world's 1.2 billion Roman Catholics.

Just a month before coming to the United States for the KCM Minister's Conference, Bishop Tony had been in Rome visiting with the man he now called "Father Francis." During the conversation Tony mentioned that he would shortly be traveling to Texas for the KCM meeting, shared how Kenneth Copeland had also played a significant role in his spiritual development, and asked if Francis would care to send him any sort of a message. Tony shared with me that he expected Fr. Francis to go to his desk and pen a short note for him to deliver privately. Pope Francis, it appears, had other ideas.

> Love God above all, and love others.

"Father Tony, do you happen to have your iPhone with you?" Francis asked.

"Yes, Father, I *always* have my iPhone." Tony replied.

"Very well," Francis said, "Then let's send him a message."

Surprised, Tony dutifully pulled out his iPhone and began to record seven minutes of loving outreach from Francis to those who would be gathering in Fort Worth, whom he addressed as his "brothers and sisters." After beginning in English with an apology that he was unable to deliver his entire message to them in English, Pope Francis explained that he would not really be speaking either Italian or English—but "heart-fully."

> It is a language more simple and authentic. This language of the heart has a special language and grammar. It is a simple grammar with two rules. Love God above all, and love others—your neighbors—because they are your brothers and sisters. With these two rules we can go ahead.

In this unlikeliest of addresses to a group of pentecostal, word-of-faith ministers and leaders, Pope Francis spoke of the two emotions occupying his heart—joy and yearning. Joy because he knew they had gathered to worship Jesus Christ as the only Lord, to pray to the Father, and to be filled with the Holy Spirit. But he also felt a yearning, because even as sometimes happens to earthly families, he recognized that they had become separated.

He went on to admit that it was a long road of sin which had caused this separation. One might have expected the Pontiff of the Roman Catholic Church to reprove the Protestants for having brought about this division and leaving the church. Instead, Francis simply acknowledged that "we share the blame," and that both sides have been sinful in their striving against one another. He was yearning, he said, for the same type of reunion that Joseph had experienced with his brothers. They had come to Egypt to buy food and instead, they found their long-lost brother. They had plenty of money; it was fraternity that they lacked.

Francis then began to pour out his heart.

> I am speaking to you as a brother. I speak to you in a simple way. With joy and yearning. Let us allow our yearning to grow, because this will propel us to find each other, to embrace one another, and together, to worship Jesus Christ as the only Lord of History.
>
> I thank you profoundly for listening to me. I thank you profoundly for allowing me to speak the language of the heart. And I also ask you a favor. Please pray for me, because I need your prayers. And I will pray for you, I will do it; but I need your prayers. And let us pray to the Lord that He unites us all. Come on, we are brothers. Let's give each other a spiritual hug and let God complete the work that he has begun. This is a miracle. The miracle of unity has begun!
>
> A famous Italian author named Manzoni once wrote in a novel of a simple man amongst the people who once said this, 'I've never seen God begin a miracle without Him finishing it well.' He will complete this miracle of unity. I ask you to bless me, and I bless you. From brother to brother, I embrace you.

From brother to brother! Staggering! Francis' invitation to unity was received and reciprocated. Copeland came to the platform and immediately led the gathering in a time of prayer for Pope Francis. Then he called Bishop Tony to the platform and recorded a message to the Pope. Five months later, Kenneth Copeland was among a group of evangelical leaders to visit the Vatican with Bishop Tony Palmer for a meeting with Pope Francis. The goal of the meeting was to begin a dialog to explore the means and basis for restoring communion between the various factions of the Body of Christ.

The men who gathered in Rome with Bishop Tony to meet Pope Francis on that day were: Kenneth Copeland, Geoff Tunnicliffe of the World Evangelical Alliance, James Robison of Life Outreach International and John Arnott of Partners in Harvest. Together they represented the vast majority of evangelical believers in the world, and they were there to discuss "John 17 unity."

The first basis upon which these men of God had come together to engage in a discussion of unity was based upon a shared commitment to the basis of their faith—salvation by grace through faith in Jesus Christ alone. It led them to agree that they were all recipients of a shared call to mission— the mission of proclaiming the gospel of Jesus Christ to the world. There it was in a nutshell. They could work together in love, on the basis of their shared faith and their common mission. These were the "essentials" upon which they agreed, and that was sufficient.

Earlier in the chapter, I promised to address the fears and claims of the detractors. These can be summarized in one overarching theme: Christian ecumenism is satanic and a precursor to the reign of the antichrist.

If the matter before us were a call to ecumenism in its broadest sense, specifically a multi-religious version of Rodney King asking, "Can't we all just get along?" (where the "all" deliberately includes non-Christians), then the charge would be accurate. And I would most certainly be on the other side of the issue. But this is precisely *not* the case at all! Rather, it is a call for intrinsic unity on the very core of the message of the gospel of Jesus Christ. It is a call for Christian communion, based upon salvation by grace through faith in Jesus Christ alone.

Communion...

The very word rings with a challenge to vibrant unity! It inspires us to consider the other members of the Body of Christ, not only in light of how they choose to relate to us, but much more importantly, with a careful examination of how we choose to relate to them. As we approach this challenge—a serious challenge to at least examine our choices in this arena, I pray that our quest allows each of us to reach higher for His empowerment, to love more deeply, and to reach our arms wide enough to recognize and accept members of the Body who choose expressions of faith and methods of worship we may find unfamiliar or foreign, yet rest squarely within the boundaries of historic orthodoxy.

Diversity is divine; it's division that is diabolic.

As we interact with those various expressions of faith and methods of worship, we would do well to remind ourselves that the goal is UNITY, not uniformity. Let's be clear, no one is suggesting that every church in every location should express their worship in exactly the same way or follow the same leaders. But, as the early church did, we need to understand that within the pale of biblical worship which is acceptable to God, there exist many different avenues of expression. As Bishop Tony Palmer said so well, "Diversity is divine; it's division that is diabolic." The apostle Paul made it abundantly clear that "the body is not made up of one part but of many." [7] In spite of his clear admonition that we cannot say we do not have need of one another, it seems we've been doing a great job of assuming precisely that very position for close to a thousand years now.

> If the foot should say, "Because I am not a hand, I do not belong to the body," it would not for that reason cease to be part of the body. And if the ear should say, "Because I am not an eye, I do not belong to the body," it would not for that reason cease to be part of the body. If the whole body were an eye, where would the sense of hearing be? If the whole body were an ear, where would the sense of smell be? But in fact God has arranged the parts in the body, every one of them, just as He wanted them to be. If they were all one part, where would the body be? As it is, there are many parts, but one body. The eye cannot say to the

---

[7] 1 Corinthians 12:14

hand, "I don't need you!" And the head cannot say to the feet, "I don't need you!" [8]

Today we tend to be more focused on who is *not* part of us, not the other way around. If Paul were writing about today's issues to the Corinthian church, he may well have written,

> If the charismatics should say, "Because you are an evangelical, you do not belong to the Body," evangelicals would not for that reason cease to be part of the Body. And if the sacramental worshippers should say, "Because you are a charismatic you do not belong to the Body," charismatics would not for that reason cease to be part of the Body.

It is so easy and normal to see that our physical body needs the diversity we find in our arms, feet, hands, eyes, and ears. Why is it so difficult for us to accept the fact that the three major historic streams of the church are designed by God to complement one another? If our physical bodies require diversity living in unity in order to function properly, how much more would this be the case for the Body of Christ?

One might try to argue against this logic and insist that his particular choices with regard to worship are *the* proper ones, except for the stubborn little fact that it is God Himself who insists on the diversity living in unity within His Body.

This is one of the things I have come to love about the convergence movement in the Church, the way that each of the historic streams maintains its own expression in a symphony of worship and adds to the others. Bishop Quintin Moore of the CEEC offered the following working definition when he said,

> The convergence movement is a coming together of the three major historic branches of the church—the sacramental, the evangelical, and the charismatic. Each of these expressions of the church of Jesus Christ has been carefully nurtured by

---
[8] 1 Corinthians 12:15–21

God and greatly used to establish, and to expand, His work on Earth. Our Lord's Prayer for His church was, "Father, that they may be one, even as we are one" (John 17:21). Ecclesiastes 4:12 tells us that "a cord of three strands is not easily broken." When the three strands of God's church are braided together there will be a new strength and unity in the church.[9]

Since we claim to be believers in Jesus Christ, it's vitally important that we consider His faith expression—how *He* worshipped.

Jesus was *sacramental*. Judaism, as it was in the time of Herod's Temple and as it remains even today after its destruction, is a sacramental religion. Moreover, the sacramental and liturgical elements, which have carried over into the Christian sacramental expression—the vestments, the liturgical modalities of prayer, and the seasonal observances of specific feasts—were prescribed and ordained by none other than God the Father Himself. Jesus followed the regulations required of Him as an observant Jew. Several of these elements of historic sacramentalism ordained by God are still observed today by Messianic followers of Yeshua. They pray many of the same blessings and prayers that have been offered by Jews throughout the centuries, and men in these congregations commonly wear the *tallit*, Judaism's classic prayer shawl. Not only that, but we clearly see from the book of Revelation that a good number of these elements will continue to play a part in our future worship in heaven, which demonstrates that God has not abandoned His love of things sacramental to reflect His glory.

Jesus was *evangelical*. His Kingdom message was unmistakably based upon an appeal to the Scriptures and a need for spiritual rebirth. Jesus insisted to Nicodemus, "You must be born again!" Jesus based His message upon the Scriptures of the Old Testament to proclaim His call to new life. He reproved the enemy by quoting, "It is written ...." He challenged His critics by demanding they try to answer difficult questions and dilemmas found in the Word of God. He stood on the prophets' teachings and showed how they referred to Him.

Jesus was *charismatic*. As "filled with the Spirit" as any of us or any among those who name the name of Christ have ever been, surely no

---

[9] What Is Convergence?, http://orderofstanthony.org/resources/

one in his right mind would claim to be more "filled" with spiritual power than Jesus. The Holy Spirit descended upon Him in bodily form when He was baptized by John, as Matthew, Mark, and Luke all bear witness. It was Jesus, after all, Who walked through the wall of the upper room in Jerusalem and instructed those gathered there to be filled with the Holy Spirit. If you remove His use of miraculous spiritual gifts from the pages of the four Gospels you are left with an empty shell of a message, not a powerful vehicle of transformational impact.

This deliberate embracing of these three historic streams, which have *always existed* in Christianity—the sacramental, the evangelical and the charismatic—is the core of the current-day convergence movement. Convergence is, at its core, a restoration of the totality of the Christian expression and a return to the fullness experienced by the early church. Even in churches that prefer to focus on one or even two of these streams, which may be totally within the will of God for that congregation, wouldn't it be healthier if they recognized and accepted other parts of the Body that choose to worship and serve the same Lord in a biblically authentic and acceptable manner? But even this would be a form of convergence.

If we are to return to unity, based on recovering the essential oneness of the first church, our walk of faith must be a constant striving to overcome—and a deliberate seeking to heal—the divisions which have separated us. It is not enough for a group to merely announce they have not emerged from divisions created by historic differences over doctrine and practice. If we ever hope to see the unity Christ prayed for in John 17, we must intentionally live the unity we claim. Our living example of unity must include an acceptance of the liturgical, the evangelical, and the charismatic, even if we don't choose to embrace them as part of our own faith life.

We must do so precisely because the Body of Christ around the globe is liturgical, evangelical, and charismatic. Not entirely, to be sure. Unquestionably, there are large elements of His Body that embrace only one or two of these aspects of Christian life. Obviously, there are even elements that emphatically reject one or the other of these streams. But the Body of Christ must be liturgical, evangelical, and charismatic, because God Himself is liturgical, evangelical, and charismatic. These elements of our faith life are only reflections of the nature of God. As such, they should be the very things that draw us together, not drive us apart.

No single element should detract from or overwhelm the others. Each historic component should be allowed to strengthen the others. As is the case with a well-prepared gourmet meal, it is the proper balance of the ingredients that allows them to complement one another. To take a concept from a unity document known as the Jerusalem Declaration,[10] we must celebrate the God-given diversity among us which enriches our global fellowship. We must acknowledge and accept freedom in secondary matters. The key is seeking the mind of Christ on any issues which threaten to divide us.

The vision for re-established unity is not limited to leaders. Among followers, disciples, and converts there are murmurs in the Body, a longing for unity. It is an intrinsic unity, one born from a desire to once again become the powerful church we read about in the Scriptures; no longer being satisfied with the so-much-less-than-powerful church we have become.

If that is going to happen, and I am convinced that it is going to happen, we must fall in love with the Jesus of the Scriptures, instead of the Jesus which many of our denominations have taught us about. We have to reach beyond the walls that separate us and stand on the foundation of the message of the gospel of Jesus Christ. Surely, Christ's gospel is a broad and solid enough foundation for us to stand upon together.

Tony Palmer's widow is a charismatic Catholic. He was an Evangelical Anglican bishop. They raised their children as Catholic Charismatic Pentecostal Evangelicals! Tony said, "When she saw that she could be Catholic, AND Charismatic, AND Evangelical, AND Pentecostal—and that it was absolutely accepted within the Catholic Church—my wife said that she'd like to re-connect her roots with her Catholic culture. So she did."

And his reasoning for this is actually a simple one—

Jesus WAS ALL OF THOSE!

---

[10] www.gafcon.org/resources/the-complete-jerusalem-statement

Chapter 2

"I Hear There are Divisions Among You"

> In the first place, I hear that when you come together as a church, there are divisions among you; and to some extent I believe it. No doubt there have to be differences among you to show which of you have God's approval.
> —1 Corinthians 11:18–19

There are voices across the spectrum of Christianity, calling for a return to the unity of the first church. Though many institutions may have become too entrenched in their ways to be able to reach outside of the walls they have built, a large and growing number of believers—including leaders of major communities and denominations—are determined to reach over, under, or around those walls of denominationalism and join hands. It is this vision to see beyond the present, by the way, which characterizes true leaders in every sphere.

But there are also other voices. There are many other people in leadership positions of churches who are *not* in favor of the steps towards unity that are being taken. They find that the walls which they have built are safer to stand behind! The divisions have become far too comfortable. While vision is supposed to be a hallmark of leadership, it is sadly not a universal trait of leaders.

When Paul wrote his first letter to the church in Corinth, one of the issues he dealt with very directly was this issue of division. He speaks about it in the first two chapters and comes back to it again and again, even in his second letter to them. In 1 Corinthians 10, he introduces his correction with the phrase "In the following directives I have no praise for you, for your meetings do more harm than good."[11] *Really*? More harm than good! It is hard to imagine a stronger rebuke from an apostle.

When we gather for our meetings without welcoming others, whoever "we" are; are we not automatically beginning to segregate "us" from "them"? I recently read a book[12] in which Daniel Tomberlin recounts an episode from his teenage years which absolutely infuriated me. In his book, he shared an incident that brought about a sharp, stern rebuke from his pastor.

You might be wondering what terrible sin he committed to merit this reprimand? Had he stolen something? Had he been found cheating or lying? Perhaps this hormonal teen had been caught in some promiscuous behavior? No, none of these sins caused his pastor's wrath. Tomberlin's egregious offense had been having the unmitigated gall to invite a young, black friend to his church—his *all-white* church—to hear the message of the gospel.

"All would have been well," Tomberlin recalls, "except he responded to the altar call to get saved. In doing so, everyone in the church became aware of his presence." So here was a young man for whom Christ had died, kneeling in repentance at the altar—only to be rebuffed and told that he was not welcome. Not because his sin was too great, but because his skin was too dark. Skin, not sin, was the issue!

I am neither a prophet nor the son of a prophet, but I can almost see the rage on the face of Christ as the offer of salvation, which cost Jesus so much, is pulled out of the pleading hands of someone who was seeking it. I don't want to be standing anywhere near that "pastor" on Judgement Day!

The immediate reaction of most people to the incident I've just shared would be justifiable shock. "Surely we've gotten past *that* today," you might be saying. On the one hand, I would say, yes. In most of our churches—at least in America—people of any color can enter freely. Though sadly,

---
[11] 1 Corinthians 11:17
[12] Pentecostal Sacraments: Encountering God at the Altar by Daniel Tomberlin

the Sunday morning worship hour still remains one of the most highly segregated times of the week. But the issue is much greater than this.

Our tendency is to think *our* meetings are good and wonderful things. Our gatherings are sacramental or are free-flowing, or orderly or evangelical, or seeker-friendly or any of a hundred other things we think are important and, therefore, assume God values very highly. While these are all good and wonderful things, the verdict of the apostle Paul is, if there is division among us, NONE of our gatherings are important, good, or wonderful, because they have become corrupted.

No love, no value.

> If I speak in the tongues of men and of angels, but have not love, I am only a resounding gong or a clanging cymbal. If I have the gift of prophecy and can fathom all mysteries and all knowledge, and if I have a faith that can move mountains, but have not love, I am nothing. If I give all I possess to the poor and surrender my body to the flames, but have not love, I gain nothing.[13]

If we have not love, even our worship services do more harm than good. It is just as true today as it was when Tomberlin's friend was turned away from the cross. How many people are turned away from Jesus today because you and I refuse to love one another? I shudder to think!

Even the very thing which is intended to unite the entire Body— the very celebration of thanksgiving instituted by the Lord Himself—does more harm than good when it is defiled by disunity. You can almost hear Paul's shock as he deals with the status quo in Corinth. It is almost as if he is shouting, "No, *that* is not the Lord's Supper! Not when some of you are so consumed in your gluttony, gorging yourselves while your brother beside you starves."

Ever the teacher, Paul then returns to the foundation of our unity:

> For I received from the Lord what I also passed on to you: The Lord Jesus, on the night He was betrayed, took bread, and

---

[13] 1 Corinthians 13:1–3

when He had given thanks, He broke it and said, "This is My body, which is for you; do this in remembrance of Me." In the same way, after supper He took the cup, saying, "This cup is the new covenant in My blood; do this, whenever you drink it, in remembrance of Me." For whenever you eat this bread and drink this cup, you proclaim the Lord's death until He comes.[14]

On the very night that He was betrayed by one of those closest to Him, Jesus took bread and gave it to those at the table with Him saying, "This is for you!" It wasn't for Himself that He had gathered the disciples around the Passover table but for them. At the table, that night, He intended to teach them lessons in grace, lessons in forgiveness, and lessons in unity. His table was meant to serve as the place—even if it was the ONLY place—where the Body could stand in its unity. The place where the Zealots could eat with the tax collectors and where those who doubted could join hands with those of strong faith. Together. At the beginning of the meal, He had filled a basin, knelt and washed everyone's feet! Jesus wanted them unified—unified by the One Whose own body and blood would purchase their ultimate unity—UNITY WITH GOD.

Will we continue to refuse the Altar and the Table on the basis of our individual preferences of styles of worship, rules, and prejudices? If we do, we do so at our own peril. How much better would loving unity be as a sign to an unbelieving world?

We get so entrenched in our own views of precisely how our Lord should be worshipped. In so doing, we erect barriers, separating ourselves from others who love Him just as much as we do, yet prefer a different expression of worship. How blind we are to believe that it is such minor things as the color of a person's skin, styles of music, modalities of preaching, or the way leaders dress, which are the critical factors in determining whether or not we should allow them to join us at our Lord's Table. We refuse the Table of Communion to those whom Christ Jesus has already accepted into His Body at the risk of His wrath.

If a person is coming to the Lord's Table by faith in Jesus Christ, why should an imperfect understanding about the precise nature of His presence

---

[14] 1 Corinthians 11:23–26

stop them? Whether he believes it to be a holy memorial or a sacramental offering, if a blood-washed believer in Jesus comes to the Table in love and faith, let the Lord lead and teach him greater truth. The wise parent does not look down at a seven-year-old child who has just told Mom or Dad he loves them and shout: "You're only seven, you have no idea what love is!" No! That would be cruel. Instead, the parent receives and accepts his juvenile expression of love for what it is—the most and best he can currently offer.

The door allowing for entrance to the Lord's Table is not a perfect understanding of the nature of the gifts! I don't know a single priest, pastor, or theologian who claims a total and complete understanding of every aspect of the nature of the Communion Table. Certainly neither the sweet first-graders making their First Holy Communion in Roman Catholic and Lutheran churches nor last month's converts in an Assembly of God or Southern Baptist church do. Allow the believer with another view on communion to join you at the Table, giving his best to the Lord and receiving all that his faith allows him to accept. And pray that a loving welcome to the blessing of the Lord's Table will bring about greater maturity, a deeper love, and a greater insight into the true nature of the Table of Christ in both of you.

If only it were matters as serious as the Communion Table that separate us! We, who are supposed to be one, have allowed ourselves to become so self-righteous that the choice of color for the hymn books or carpet has been sufficient grounds to split a congregation that has been worshipping together for decades. When we allow that, are we any less wrong than Tomberlin's pastor? Are we any less deserving of Paul's rebuke that our meetings do more harm than good?

How is it that we miss the key thing that matters most?

If anyone is in Christ, he is a new creation; the old has gone, the new has come![15]

How have we dared to add our own criteria to the only one that Jesus has established—"IN CHRIST"? The old, sinful man, the one who was truly separated from God, has been recreated into a new man! No more

---
[15] 2 Corinthians 5:17

separation, no more division. The Almighty One, choosing to reconcile the world to Himself, through Christ, and to make us one—this is the only thing that truly matters.

IN CHRIST! That is the standard to apply. He is the foundation of our unity.

If we be found in Christ, what other basis for unity must be attained? If Christ has accepted, re-created, and sealed someone, who are we to set a different standard? How is it that we dare to build barricades around His Table, as though it were our own? How do we set up a standard He did not when He died to include His children in the feast of Thanksgiving? That's what the word *Eucharist* means—*thanksgiving*.

> If Christ has accepted, re-created, and sealed someone, who are we to set a different standard?

It's His family Table, where everyone who is in Christ ought to be welcomed and loved so they can join in giving thanks for His indescribable gift.

"Because there is one loaf, we, who are many, are one body, for we all partake of the one loaf."[16] Of course we are many, but we are also one. Our unity is intrinsic in our salvation. The greatest barrier to true unity—our sin—has been removed by the cross. "God made him who had no sin to be sin for us, so that in him we might become the righteousness of God."[17] As we will examine in greater detail in chapter four, this salvation is by grace through faith in Jesus Christ and His sacrifice. It is freely offered. It is totally based upon Him, not us. So it is rather artificial for anyone who has received so great a gift, as the very forgiveness of their sin, to add requirements that the Savior Himself did not, don't you think?

Some time ago, I had the opportunity to spend several hours in Rome with Pope Francis. (I recognize that this fact alone is enough for some who are reading this to draw back and want to erect a barrier!) It was a small, intimate gathering, which allowed for extended conversation and discussion. This was my first meeting with the Pope since the death of Bishop Tony Palmer. During our time together, Pope Francis related a story

---

[16] 1 Corinthians 10:17
[17] 2 Corinthians 5:21

that Bishop Tony had shared with him from his childhood, growing up as white child in South Africa.

"Bishop Tony told me that there were white and black children in the schools," Pope Francis shared. "They would walk to school together. They would learn together. They would play together. But at the time for the hour of the meal, they would be forced to segregate. And they would say, 'We want to eat together,' but it would not be allowed."

Francis paused at that point to reflect for a moment, and then he said, "That hunger has continued. We should walk together; we should eat together from the Table of the Lord, the way the Lord wants—and wills."

The Lord does indeed want us to walk together, and to eat together! It is in our UNITY that His glory is displayed. The divisiveness in our house brings us shame. Even worse, the powerlessness this division causes in the Church brings *Him* shame. In allowing ourselves to erect artificial barriers between our denominations and churches, we have built barriers for the gospel to a world that desperately needs Jesus.

The apostle's admonition echoes through the centuries. "I hear there are divisions among you." Yes, Paul, sadly this is still true. We haven't learned yet.

Bishop's Tony's experience as a child of apartheid could become a valuable lesson for us. There was a time in South Africa when no one could have foreseen a black man sitting and eating with a white man. It wasn't long ago that the one saw separate toilets, water fountains, restaurants, and schools for "colored" people in the Southern United States. Both in Cape Town and Atlanta, those days are long gone. While no one would claim that every issue between the races has been resolved, at least we are able to sit at the same table in a restaurant.

> How can it be that the world allows for a greater unity than the Church?

How can it be that the world allows for a greater unity than the Church? We have a greater call to unity…a greater mission to accomplish.

> If anyone is in Christ, he is a new creature; the old things passed away; behold, new things have come. Now all these

> things are from God, *who reconciled us to Himself through Christ* and gave us the ministry of reconciliation, namely, that God was in Christ reconciling the world to Himself, not counting their trespasses against them, and He has committed to us the word of reconciliation. Therefore, we are ambassadors for Christ, as though God were making an appeal through us; we beg you on behalf of Christ, be reconciled to God. He made Him who knew no sin to be sin on our behalf, so that we might become the righteousness of God in Him.[18] (Emphasis added)

Paul would beg pagans, on Christ's behalf, to be reconciled to God. On Christ's behalf, I am begging you—who claim to have been reconciled to God—will you not be reconciled to one another? We cannot remain separate and divided when we have been tasked with such an awesome call. We've been told that our *love* is the sign the world will use to know whether or not we are truly His disciples. We have been given the ministry of reconciling a sinful world to a Holy God! We cannot remain aloof from the present situation, while a world without Christ spins into a hopeless eternity. Jesus said,

> My prayer is not for them alone. I pray also for those who will believe in Me through their message, that all of them may be one, Father, just as You are in Me and I am in You. May they also be in Us so that the world may believe that You have sent Me. I have given them the glory that You gave Me, that they may be one as We are one: I in them and You in Me. May they be brought to complete unity to let the world know that You sent Me and have loved them even as You have loved Me.[19]

We live in a time where we experience levels of evil that have never before been seen by the world at large. Hardly a day goes by that we do not see an expression of evil, worse than the day before, blast itself across our television or computer screen. In recent memory, we have seen a dozen

---

[18] 2 Corinthians 5:17–21 (NASB)
[19] John 17:20–23

people massacred for printing a cartoon. As if this were not bad enough, the following week Muslim militants provided us with photos of ten- to twelve-year-old boys murdering bound prisoners whose only crime was their belief in Jesus Christ. Seven coordinated attacks in Paris took the lives of 130 innocent victims and injured three times that number. One terrorist snuffed out the lives of close to fifty people in Orlando, in the worst mass shooting incident in US history. The list could go on and on and on. (And by the time your read these words, it most likely has!)

WHERE IS THE GLORY OF GOD? Where is the massive and powerful church, unified by the blood of the Lamb, standing together with the power that manifests the Almighty's glory and impacts the unsaved world around us? Has our light become so dim as to become ineffective in eradicating the darkness that surrounds us? Light is supposed to overcome darkness!

Christ interceded for all of us, that we would be ONE. He prayed, "That all of them may be one, Father, just as You are in Me and I am in You. May they also be in Us." But there was a reason for His prayer. He continued, "so that the world may believe that You have sent Me." SO THAT! One outcome of our unity will be the conviction of the world that the Father did, indeed, send Jesus to pay the price for our sins on the cross. The manifestation of this unity was the visible glory of God, being seen in the ministry of those who proclaimed Christ. "I have given them the glory that You gave Me, that they may be one as We are one: I in them and You in Me."

The damning fact is that we have abandoned the glory of God by refusing to maintain the unity of the Spirit in the bonds of peace.[20] We have become so determined to proclaim the supposed errors of our brothers that we have abandoned the glory, which comes from proclaiming the gospel of our Lord.

Even a cursory reading of the Acts of the Apostles presents the reader with an undeniable fact. The glory of God being manifest in the day-to-day ministry of the believers was seen in signs in the heavens above and wonders on the earth below. The dead were raised, sick healed, lepers cleansed, liars stuck down (and sent to their graves), and opponents of the gospel were struck blind. In Christ's prayer, He, Himself, tied our unity to the display of God's glory. This was no accident. The walls we build between us block

---

[20] Ephesians 4:3

the flow of the glory and power of God, because He has ordained that His glory be seen in our unity.

It was wonderful that so many world leaders gathered in Paris to march together in a show of global solidarity in the face of Islamic terrorism. Can you imagine with me what the outcome might have been if a unified church had come together in Paris—believers from forty plus different denominations—instead of leaders from forty plus different nations. Imagine if these unified members of the Body of Christ had prayed over the slain and seen them returned to life. How many more millions would have marched in the streets of Paris behind a dozen who had been raised from the dead by the prayer of a unified church?

"Impossible!" you say.

"Of course!" I agree. "That's the point." Is that not the very definition of a miracle? If the dead can be raised in Papua, New Guinea, then why not in Paris, France?

Signs in the heavens above and wonders on the earth below are the very things that display the glory of God. It is their very impossibility that draws attention to them and grabs the attention of those who do not yet believe in Christ.

Your particular faith tradition may not accept the continuing operation of the miraculous. You may have been taught that the day of miracles ended with the death of the apostles. But I would ask, even if you choose to walk out your faith without experiencing the miraculous, *is that a license for division*? Has the glory of God come to an end? With or without a belief that the age or the miraculous continues, has the need for all of us, who are saved by grace, to proclaim the good news of Christ ceased? Rather than argue or separate over such a question, would we not be better servants by standing UNITED IN CHRIST and then seeing what He does? Would our Lord not be better served if we were to stand together and fulfill whatever particular role He calls us to?

We are called to be one Body. But we would do well to keep in mind the simple fact that different parts of the body do different things. If the hand is not "comfortable" doing what the foot is called to do, I say, "Of course not! Why would you even expect that it would be?" If the eye is unable to do what the ear is called to do, are we surprised? Is the eye then any less useful?

The unfortunate truth is that the feet among us become easily offended when the elbows refuse to serve like feet. And the eyes refuse to see any value in the hands serving differently from them. How is it that we can all see the foolishness in these silly little illustrations, but thousands of denominations (and sadly, yes, there are thousands of them) cannot apply the lesson to their own body. "In the same way, even though we are many people, we are one body in the Messiah and individual parts connected to each other."[21]

> Our diversity is supposed to be our strength, not a cause for division.

Our diversity is supposed to be our strength, not a cause for division. The world could not ignore the impact of a united body of Christ, standing together and being the light and salt we were called to be. If we stood together while hands were hands, feet were feet, and each part of the body did its part, we would soon turn the world upside down! It wouldn't be the first time.[22]

Paul wrote, "We implore you on Christ's behalf: Be reconciled to God."[23]

If we truly discern the Body, we will see that He has made us one. And if black and white men can see that they are actually one race—the human race, perhaps it is not too great a reach to hope that God can open our eyes to discern the Body and see our oneness, too. I implore you on Christ's behalf: Be reconciled to one another.

It is high time for the Body of Christ to become deliberate about unity!

---

[21] Romans 12:5 (ISV)
[22] Acts 17:16
[23] 2 Corinthians 5:20

Chapter 3

Discerning the Body

Perhaps we can draw a lesson or two from believers who have embraced the Convergence Movement. Believers currently worshipping in a convergence church probably have a greater opportunity to experience a balance of the sacramental, the evangelical, and the charismatic. This balance is intended to connect believers to heaven by means of powerful charismatic worship, leading to biblically-grounded life and growth by means that include liturgy and the Eucharist. The power of converging these streams in the unity of the Body could have as significant an impact as it does for congregations, communions, and denominations that embrace all three historic streams. As acceptance continues to be embraced on a broader basis, more and more Christians who have walked in one or two of these expressions may begin to embrace the fullness of the three streams in their own lives.

What do the various elements of look like? How do they "fit together?" Does fitting them together allow us to discern the body of Christ more fully? Before we examine some specific elements that have characterized convergence churches, congregations, denominations, and communions, perhaps an examination of the individual elements and the characteristics that define them would be of value.

A sacramental church is one that believes the sacraments are outward and visible signs that convey an inward and spiritual grace. This grace is given by Christ to His Body, the Church.

The definition of the word "sacrament" originated with Augustine in the 400s, when he described a sacrament as "the visible form of an invisible grace." Though not the exclusive means of grace, sacraments are a means by which we continually receive renewed expressions of His grace and love toward us, as we participate in them. Participating in the sacraments strengthens the believers in their innermost being, because God's grace is conveyed through the sacraments to His Church. In other words, the impartation of grace is an act of God, not an act of man.

Sacramental worshippers hold the belief that, through their use of the liturgy in worship, they are better able to include the entire gathered body of believers in their expression of love to our Creator and Savior. This is because participating in the liturgy allows every member of the Body of Christ to live out their God-ordained role as priest. Peter tells believers that we are all "a chosen people, a royal priesthood, a holy nation, a people belonging to God," and by the exercise of that royal priesthood we "declare the praises of Him who called (us) out of darkness into His wonderful light."[24] Sacramental churches draw their worship practices and liturgy from different points of time—from Orthodox or Catholic expressions of faith and practice, to the practices of the Protestant Reformation. Sacramentally-focused congregations frequently have an altar in a position of prominence at the front of their churches. Sacramental worship aims to draw from the liturgical beauty found in both the Eastern and Western expressions of Christian worship.

Holding to "the faith once delivered unto the saints,"[25] an evangelical church would unequivocally declare their belief that the Holy Scriptures of the Old and New Testaments are the inspired Word of God. They contain all things necessary for salvation and godly living. Evangelicals would hold to the historic and conservative position that Scripture is the inerrant and inspired Word of God Himself and, as such, the Scriptures are a faithful guide in all matters.

Evangelical churches see the Holy Scriptures as the sole rule of faith and practice, often acknowledging their need to be interpreted by historic orthodoxy, reason, and experience. Though denominations exist which claim to stand upon *sola scriptura* (the scriptures alone), even these branches of Christianity often make widespread use of commentaries and the writings

---

[24] 1 Peter 2:9
[25] Jude 3

and teaching of their founders, as well. Sacred tradition, it seems, is difficult to avoid entirely. These churches fully embrace the historic orthodoxy of the two primary Christian creeds, commonly called the Apostles' Creed and the Nicene Creed. Though they may not make use of the Creed of Saint Athanasius, which provides a doctrinal statement on the divinity of Jesus, most would have no objection to its content.

Evangelicals hold that the teachings of the Bible are not subject to the whimsy of modern society, nor should our application of them be. Precisely because they hold to such a high view of Holy Scripture, they are committed to the faithful reading, studying, teaching, and preaching from them and that, often, systematically. Since evangelicals accept the Scriptures as the very Word of God, these churches believe they are the wellspring of spiritual maturity. Evangelically-focused congregations frequently have their pulpit in a position of prominence at the front of their churches.

Recognizing that the Church has always had a responsibility to identify and reject both heretical teachings and those who embrace them, biblical evangelicals have historically based their standards of behavior and conduct on the teachings of Scripture. Any decision to stand within the pale of historic orthodoxy will require the church not stand with those who have abandoned it.

Those who embrace the evangelical distinctiveness share a key understanding of the importance of a personal relationship with Jesus Christ, living a holy life, and a commitment to evangelism and missions. In a word, they are not ashamed of the gospel. They recognize that Jesus Christ is the only hope for man's salvation. "Salvation is found in no one else, for there is no other name under heaven given to men by which we must be saved."[26]

A Spirit-filled charismatic church would hold to the position that they must be open to the continuing work, gifts, and ministry of the Holy Spirit. As Eddie Hyatt has documented in his book *2000 Years of Charismatic Christianity*,[27] God's people have always been a spiritually gifted people. From the early apostles to the modern church, Christians have been endowed with a power beyond themselves, the *dunamis* power of the Holy

---

[26] Acts 4:12
[27] *2000 Years Of Charismatic Christianity: A 21st Century Look At Church History From A Pentecostal/Charismatic Prospective*. Eddie L Hyatt

Spirit. I have often held up my Bible while preaching and asked, "What do you read in this book that convinces you that God called you to do the possible?" A charismatic church sees it as their calling to bring the power of Christ into direct contact with the needs of the world and thereby, show the glory of God.

Charismatic churches point out that the Holy Spirit's power is such a critical element for effective ministry that those who had been trained and discipled by Jesus Himself were forbidden to begin their ministry immediately after His ascension into heaven. Christ's final command to His disciples was absolutely clear—they were to remain in Jerusalem until they had received the power of the indwelling Holy Spirit. Even three years of training at the hands of Jesus Himself was insufficient to prepare them to take His message to the world. They needed the indwelling Holy Spirit.

Charismatic believers would insist that His indwelling presence and the accompanying power of His gifts of grace are as much a requirement for effective ministry today as they were then. Surely, we cannot think we have the power to transform lives in and of ourselves! So we must constantly seek the infilling power of God in our lives.

Paul's directive in Ephesians 5:18 is stated in the present infinitive tense. He instructs us to "be constantly being filled with the Spirit." Charismatically-focused congregations frequently have an open area for Spirit-empowered prayer in a position of prominence at the front of their churches. Further, charismatic congregations would insist upon the need to encourage, to allow, and anticipate the Holy Spirit's presence and working through the spiritual gifts—in their worship services, as well as daily acts of service, and in personal relationship with Him.

Whichever of these three streams of understanding and practice we find ourselves participating in, we must concede the certain knowledge that few things are as clearly commanded in Scripture as the *absolute unity* of the Body of Christ. As we have seen, Paul wrote that there is "one body and one Spirit—just as you were called to one hope when you were called—one Lord, one faith, one baptism; one God and Father of all, who is over all and through all and in all."[28] The unquestionable command to every Christian is to "make every effort to keep the unity of the Spirit through the bond of

---
28 Ephesians 4:4–6

peace."[29] Paul's instruction to "make every effort" should be understood as a mandate commanding us to reach out in love, to build bridges and relationships with our brothers and sisters in Christ, wherever and whenever we can.

We must refuse to see ourselves in competition with other believers, churches, groups, communions, denominations, or movements. How can you possibly be in competition with yourself? There is ONE BODY. The hand is not better than the ear because it serves a different function. The left eye does not compete with the kidney, nor can it do so. It doesn't even compete with the right eye. Both eyes working together are needed for optimal depth perception and balance.

> How can you possibly be in competition with yourself? There is ONE BODY.

We are all members of one body. As each of us walks out our calling, our goal is only to "use whatever gift he has received to serve others, faithfully administering God's grace in its various forms" in order that "in all things God may be praised through Jesus Christ."[30]

Completion is a much better view than competition. The foot completes the body, so the hand can reach goals which benefit the entire body. They fulfill totally different functions, yet accomplish far more together than they ever could apart. A sacramental congregation based in Nashville, Tennessee, is not "in competition" with the Southern Baptist Convention, though the SBC is headquartered there. They are two parts of one body. A charismatic church based in London, England, is not "in competition" with Canterbury. They support and complement one another. An evangelical congregation in Springfield, Missouri, is not "in competition" with the Assemblies of God. They each serve the same Lord. Each reaches some, none reaches all, but together we can reach more.

I believe that is far past time to put the concept of competition to death. We *are* the Body of Christ, whether we choose to accept and properly act upon that fact or not. Note, please, the Scriptures speak of us as THE body. There is only one!

---

29 Ephesians 4:3
30 1 Peter 4:10-11

> God has combined the members of the body and has given greater honor to the parts that lacked it, *so that there should be no division in the body*, but that its parts should have equal concern for each other. If one part suffers, every part suffers with it; if one part is honored, every part rejoices with it. Now you are the body of Christ, and each one of you is a part of it.[31] (Emphasis added)

Did you catch that? God has *combined* the members of the Body of Christ. Each one of us is a part, yet only a part. If we are to accomplish the task set before us, each part must do its part. Moreover, He has done so and instructed us that "there should be *no division*" in this wonderful Body He has chosen to create. Fulfill the role God gave YOU, and support your brothers and sisters in the role God gave them.

Let me try to forestall the objections some will likely raise—concerns of wild ecumenism based upon nothing more than some well-intentioned desire for unity. I am not describing unity with Muslims, Mormons, Jews, Buddhists, or any other person or group outside the historic Christian faith. I am speaking wholly and entirely about people who are in Christ, and who acknowledge Him as Savior. The next chapter addresses this topic in great detail. For now, I would just ask the following question: If Jesus Himself says a person is in Christ, on what basis do we dare say he is not? Or, to phrase it a bit differently, if He invites people to His Table, on what basis could we possibly choose to exclude them from fellowship or the Lord's Supper? Isn't the final arbiter of who is in Christ…well, CHRIST?

It is time that we extend fellowship and communion to our Christian brothers and sisters—those who are in Christ by virtue of their faith in Him—whatever denominations, churches, or synods they may choose to worship in; instead of being like the prodigal's older brother, standing outside of His feast of thanksgiving and refusing to enter. We, who have been commanded to love one another, must be committed to the unity of all those who know and love Christ. We must be committed to building authentic relationships within the Body of Christ.

---

[31] 1 Corinthians 12:24–27

Shouldn't we look for opportunities to pray with and for one another? Shouldn't we decide to stand alongside each other and support each part of the Body as it fulfills the role to which God called it? Why do we have such difficulty seeing that the hand cannot possibly fulfill the role of the eye and only disaster awaits if it tries. We must be determined to learn to *Count to One*. It is the only way we can succeed.

When will we begin to extend open arms to those in the Body of Christ who accept freely and conform willingly to the essential principles of the gospel, but who choose a different worship expression than we do? We must celebrate and affirm biblical and anointed spiritual ministry throughout the world to everyone. There is only *"one faith, one hope, and one baptism, one God, and Father of us all."* There is one Head, Jesus Christ, and one pure Body of Christ, the Church. We must commit to the path of unity in the bond of peace, whether someone stands within our particular denomination or alongside us in theirs, so long as they are IN CHRIST.

As has been so well said in the vision statement of Life Church, "We do not exist for the church. We *are* the Church, and we exist for the world."[32] The world *needs* to hear the gospel. But, the sad fact is, we have proven utterly ineffective in completing the Great Commission as a divided entity, at odds with ourselves.

Abba Eban, an Israeli diplomat who served as Israel's Ambassador to the United States, once observed, "History shows that men and nations behave reasonably only when they have exhausted all other alternatives." We are now some two thousand years into the mission Jesus delivered to us, and we have become divided into well over 33,000 denominations, synods, assemblies, communions, churches, and fellowships. Have we not yet exhausted all other alternatives? We have focused inwardly for too long to try and make every part of the Body like us.

I have a novel idea: How about choosing unity?

The fact of the matter is that, when we accept the offer of grace from Jesus and are adopted into His family, we find ourselves now suddenly grafted into a family of others who have accepted the same offer of forgiveness. Unfortunately, for us, most of these others are very different from ourselves. Sure, we're part of the family of God. Of course we are ONE

---

[32] www.thelifechurch.com/pages/vision-values

BODY. But it's the differences that drive us to distraction, the differences that end up dividing us.

Revelation 8:1 tells us that when the seventh seal is opened, there will be silence in heaven for about a half hour. One preacher jokingly observed that perhaps that occurs when we all begin to look around heaven, see everyone else who is there and are shocked into abject silence, especially when we observe those we were convinced were NEVER in the Body.

In chapter five, we'll look at one of the major historical foundations upon which the Church was able to stand together for the best part of one thousand years—the Nicene Creed. And we'll consider how this ancient principle may be a door for beginning a new era of communication, understanding, and trust among believers in Jesus. But, for now, let's just think about the impact that a truly united Body of Christ could have on this world, standing together in one spirit for the sake of the gospel!

The Jesus we find in the Bible promises to welcome us into a love-relationship with the Almighty Creator of the universe, based upon the forgiveness He purchased for us on the cross. And then, He calls us to follow Him in a relationship that will become the greatest treasure in our lives. That's the message of the Book of Books—when you fall totally in love with Him, everything else becomes less and less important (even the issues which we have allowed to separate us for hundreds of years).

As for our differences, we can move past them. We can discuss them and gain greater understanding of one another's beliefs. We can offer liberty in non-essential matters. Perhaps we can even (gasp) change some of our own opinions about certain matters as we grow and develop! But we do not have to accept forced changes, we can continue to be diverse—the way we were *designed* to be.

The apostle Paul said, "For me to live is CHRIST, and to die is GAIN"[33] (emphasis added). Can we say the same thing? Have you come to the point in your walk with Jesus where He has become everything to you? Where you'd give up anything for Him? Is His love the driving force in your life and the main characteristic of who you are?

Jesus Himself tells us the parable of someone who finds a treasure hidden in a field and then joyfully sells everything he has to buy the field,

---

[33] Philippians 1:21

because the treasure is worth it all.[34] Those of us who are in Christ can say, "I've found a love that is greater than life itself, a love that draws me closer to the One I love and at the same time drives me out of my comfort zone to serve Him in unity with my brothers and sisters in Christ."

I love the way Pastor Francis Chan describes the response of someone who sees Christ as the treasure who becomes his life and all in all—the One for Whom he will give up everything. He says,

> I gave up a lot to follow Jesus, but living for Him is something so good, now I am so consumed with Him that everything I do is Jesus! It is like a guy finding a treasure in a field, and going: "No way!! I can have that?!" And with great joy he sells everything he has to get that field. God says, "I am that great, and I expect you to see me as that great."
>
> Where you say, "Wow! Are you kidding me?! I can actually fall in love with the one who created me? This is a joke right? The one who created me wants to be in a love relationship with me? Are you kidding me?! The one who created me, who made this whole world and actually had His one and only Son actually come and die on a cross to pay the price for everything I did that was offensive to him! And now He wants to love me and have an eternal relationship with me?
>
> He sits on the throne—I can have him?! Wow, where do I sign up?"[35]

When we acknowledge His lordship, He welcomes us into His family and we are reborn in Him. We are reborn into His family—a family that includes all of the others across the globe, and throughout time, all who ever have and ever will make the choice to receive Him, becoming one *in Christ*. Yes, ALL of them! I believe it is absurd to think that any one of us (or any group of us)—small, unimportant, created beings—should have the audacity to place our opinions above the judicial decision of the Almighty Creator of all, Who was and is and is to come.

---

[34] Matthew 13:44
[35] Pastor Francis Chan sermon "Living Courageously"

COUNT TO ONE

Our Lord, our Savior, our Master and Creator, commands us to be one. He insists that we live our lives standing with one another, contending for the gospel. Words like *command* and *insist* don't sit well with some of us. We prefer the westernized, limp-wristed, and effeminate Jesus we see portrayed in movies—the Jesus who would never demand we change our ways to conform to His. Perhaps we would do well to remember that He is the One Who reproved Peter on a Jaffa rooftop and told Peter not to dare call unclean what He had pronounced clean.

Paul, the apostle, speaks about this in his letter to the Philippians. He writes:

> Whatever happens, conduct yourselves in a manner worthy of the gospel of Christ. Then, whether I come and see you or only hear about you in my absence, I will know that you stand firm in one spirit, contending as one man for the faith of the gospel without being frightened in any way by those who oppose you. This is a sign to them that they will be destroyed, but that you will be saved—and that by God.[36]

Let me ask you a question. What do you think it would it look like if we were all standing firm in one spirit?

I confess, my initial response to this thought was that it would be very hard to even imagine what it would look like. But then a different answer dawned on me. I realized that we don't have to imagine it at all! We have the inspired historical account of the book of Acts showing us precisely what it would look like.

I'll be the first to admit that the biblical picture of the Church in the first forty days after the resurrection isn't exactly awe inspiring. The end of the gospels and the first chapter of Acts show us how low the tide of faith had left the harbor. In the forty days after His resurrection, Jesus' apostles

---

[36] Philippians 1:27–29

DISCERNING THE BODY

had left Jerusalem and returned to the Galilee, totally confused about what their next steps should be.

John 21 gives us a glimpse into their despair. After sitting around for weeks, with no clear direction or word from Jesus recorded in the Scriptures, Peter throws in the towel and announces that he is going back to fishing. Many of us miss the serious implication of what Peter said. For us, it's no big deal for someone to take a day off and relax by a quiet stream with a fishing pole. Nowadays, lots of backsliders go fishing. But in those days, fishing was not a recreational activity. It was exclusively a commercial pursuit or subsistence activity. Peter had just told the men he had lived with for three years, "I quit! I don't know about you guys, but I've got to make a living." To make matters worse, the other apostles had said, "Yeah. Let's go." It was a mass exodus of the key men who had been trained by the Messiah. And the fate of the world literally hung in the balance. If these men were not going to proclaim the gospel, mankind was utterly without hope. There was no Plan B.

After fishing all night with nothing to show for it, they are surely discouraged and frustrated. In an ironic conversation, reminiscent of the one recorded in Luke 5, Jesus shows up and asks if they have caught anything. (As if He didn't already know!) After hearing their negative reply, He instructs them to throw out their net on the right side of the boat, and He promises they'll find fish. It is as if the Lord was saying, "You're on the wrong side of this issue, fellas. Why don't you try throwing the net on the *right side* and see what happens?" We all know the outcome. They caught more fish than could be hauled in. John blurts out, "It is the Lord!" And I can just about imagine Peter retorting, "Ya think, John-boy!?"

After breakfast, Jesus takes Peter for a walk and presents him with the choice of a lifetime. Jesus makes it clear to Peter that his present love is the real issue, not his previous failures. He invites him back into the ministry of the gospel. In effect, Jesus tells Peter to forget about fishing, it's all about shepherding. Peter needs to be about the task of feeding and caring for the sheep.

Oh, and by the way, it was also time to stop running away from Jerusalem, the Chief Priests, the Sanhedrin and the Romans. "He gave them this command: 'Do not leave Jerusalem, but wait for the gift my Father promised, which you have heard me speak about. For John baptized with water, but in a few days you will be baptized with the Holy Spirit.'"[37] Jesus apparently sent them back, because that's where we find them in Acts 1.

Once they had returned to Jerusalem, Jesus appeared to them once again. Everyone was sitting around in the same house where the Lord had shared the Last Supper with them, and all of a sudden, Jesus joined them. The next thing they knew, He was leading them out for a walk to the Mount of Olives.

It must have felt like the good-old-days, as they walked through the narrow streets of the Old City of Jerusalem, across the Kidron Valley, past the Garden of Gethsemane, and up to the top of the Mount of Olives. They'd walked this way before, so perhaps they felt that things were finally getting back to normal. So normal, in fact, that it was time to ask Jesus about His Kingdom.

> Then they gathered around him and asked him, "Lord, are you at this time going to restore the kingdom to Israel?" He said to them: "It is not for you to know the times or dates the Father has set by his own authority. But you will receive power when the Holy Spirit comes on you; and you will be My witnesses in Jerusalem, and in all Judea and Samaria, and to the ends of the earth." After He said this, He was taken up before their very eyes, and a cloud hid Him from their sight.[38]

Ten days later, on the Feast of Pentecost, God filled all those gathered in the upper room with the Holy Spirit. The day of empowerment for their mission had finally come. And with it, came the equipping Jesus had told them to wait for, a holy boldness to begin proclaiming His message. Those crowded in the upper room were instantly transformed. This band of people, who had been cowering in fear behind locked doors only a few short weeks before, became a *unified* body of powerful men and women, unafraid of anyone or anything—and who could be stopped by nothing.

---

[37] Acts 1:4–5
[38] Acts 1:6–9

Peter stepped forward and began to preach, and three thousand people got saved and were baptized. But it was not some homogenous group of Orthodox Jews from a single synagogue who were converted, as though THAT might have made it easier for everyone to get along with one another. No, these were "Parthians, Medes and Elamites; residents of Mesopotamia, Judea and Cappadocia, Pontus and Asia, Phrygia and Pamphylia, Egypt and the parts of Libya near Cyrene; visitors from Rome (both Jews and converts to Judaism); Cretans and Arabs."[39]

I think it is safe to say that you'd be hard pressed to find a more diverse group with whom to start a new church! So what was the outcome of this hodge-podge, you may wonder? Did they begin to argue and squabble with one another? Or did they perhaps segregate into different denominations and insist on following their own historical modes of worship? Surely, at least the Jews and the Arabs went in different directions, right? Not hardly. "They devoted themselves to the apostles' teaching and to the fellowship, to the breaking of bread and to prayer."[40]

And people were being added to the Kingdom every day!

They were standing firm in one spirit. EVERYBODY shared EVERYTHING. None of them claimed anything was their own. They worshipped together. Together! In spite of the cultural differences between them. They met in one another's homes, shared meals and fellowship. In the midst of all this, the apostles performed a large number of miracles, signs, and wonders. I don't believe those two elements are unrelated. When Jesus prayed for us on the night of His passion, He said that He had given the apostles the glory the Father had given Him, "that they may be one." This glory would result in greater unity, and THEN the world would know that the Father had sent His Son into the world, and that the Father loves them.

As they stood firm in one spirit, they became unstoppable. God continued to perform miracles, signs, and wonders, which attracted people to the message of the gospel of Christ. They stood together in determined unity of the Body of Christ.

And *more* people were being added to the Kingdom every day!

In Acts 3, Peter and John prayed for a man who was lame from birth,

---
[39] Acts 2:9–11
[40] Acts 2:42

and God healed him. The man was dancing and leaping around in the temple courts, rejoicing in his healing, and this naturally attracted quite a crowd.

> Peter saw his opportunity and addressed the crowd. "People of Israel," he said, "what is so surprising about this? And why stare at us as though we had made this man walk by our own power or godliness? Through faith in the name of Jesus, this man was healed—and you know how crippled he was before. Faith in Jesus' name has healed him before your very eyes."[41]

And *even more* people were added to the Kingdom that day!

In Acts 4, the priests, the captain of the temple guard, and the Sadducees get into the picture, very upset because the apostles were proclaiming the gospel. The next day, Peter and John are brought before an assembly of the highest magnitude to face their accusations. It included the rulers, the elders, and all the teachers of the law in Jerusalem. Acts 4:6 tells us that Annas, the high priest, was there, and so were Caiaphas, John, Alexander, and others of the high priest's family. This group would have sent the pre-Pentecost apostles scurrying for cover in fear. But that was then, this is now, and Peter was in rare form! He proclaimed the name of Jesus, and even went so far as to proclaim to the teachers of Israel that "salvation is found in NO ONE ELSE!"[42] (Emphasis added)

The high priest, the gathered Sanhedrin, and the assembled leaders commanded them to stop teaching and preaching this message. But the church was standing firm in one spirit, and the apostles were NOT swayed by these threats. In fact, they were emboldened. Once they were released, Peter and John went back to the church and reported what had happened. The believers began to pray…together. The content of their prayer is remarkable. They didn't pray for protection. They didn't pray for a way out of Jerusalem. They didn't even pray to be taken up to heaven to be with Jesus.

They asked for *more boldness*!

---

[41] Acts 3:12, 16 (NLT)
[42] Acts 4:12

Now, Lord, consider their threats and enable your servants to speak your word with great boldness. Stretch out your hand to heal and perform miraculous signs and wonders through the name of your holy servant Jesus. After they prayed, the place where they were meeting was shaken. And they were all filled with the Holy Spirit and spoke the word of God boldly.[43]

Hey, Lord, they're threatening to beat us and lock us all in prison. So give us MORE BOLDNESS, pour forth MORE MIRACLES, give them MORE SIGNS, and show MORE WONDERS. We don't care about us, Lord, just give us MORE GRACE to maintain the unity of the Spirit in the bond of peace, and let the name of Jesus be lifted up!

And *still more* people were being added to the Kingdom!

Acts 4:32 reiterates that "all the believers were one in heart and mind." The church was unstoppable so long as it maintained its unity. In the face of many valid reasons to allow for division, the Church determined to stand together in unity. Nothing could divide them, and therefore, nothing could stop them.

In Acts 5, the enemy tries to divide them with greed. But God takes the lives of Ananias and Saphira, preserves the unity of the Church, and they continue to proclaim the gospel. In Acts 5:14, we read that "more and more men and women believed in the Lord and were added to their number." Even though the apostles were flogged for preaching Jesus, they decided to stand firm in one spirit—TOGETHER! They were unstoppable. "Day after day, in the temple courts and from house to house, they never stopped teaching and proclaiming the good news that Jesus is the Christ."[44]

In Acts 7, the enemy tries to sow dissention in the Church, and the Grecian Jews complained that the Hellenistic Jews were being overlooked in the distribution of charity. The apostles didn't create two denominations and hope the Grecian Jews would finally be able to get along with themselves. They addressed the matter, ensured unity and equity and moved on with the proclamation of the gospel. "The number of believers greatly increased in Jerusalem, and many of the Jewish priests were converted, too."[45]

---
[43] Acts 4:29–31
[44] Acts 5:42
[45] Acts 6:7 (NLT)

Yes, you guessed it, *still more and more* people were being added to the Kingdom!

I could go on and on through the rest of the book of Acts, but you get the point. The early Church became an unstoppable force because they were determined to stand in unity, or as Paul put it, they "stood firm in one spirit." They recognized that the Body of Christ was to *Count to One* and embrace their oneness, all the while adamantly refusing to allow division.

It is not that they lacked opportunities to allow division to enter. The enemy attacked them with lies, persecution, threats from authority, floggings, dissention from within, and with the all-out attack of the Jewish religious leaders. But no matter what happened, they determined to conduct themselves in a manner worthy of the gospel of Christ, contending as one man for the faith.

Let's re-read Paul's admonition to the Philippians:

> Whatever happens, conduct yourselves in a manner worthy of the gospel of Christ. Then, whether I come and see you or only hear about you in my absence, I will know that you stand firm in one spirit, contending as one man for the faith of the gospel without being frightened in any way by those who oppose you. This is a sign to them that they will be destroyed, but that you will be saved—and that by God.[46]

WHATEVER HAPPENS

Of course things are going to happen! We are people who make mistakes and who have feelings. Stepping on one another's toes is inevitable. Worse than that, we have an enemy who is out to destroy the work of God. Lots of things are going to happen, and on the surface of it, any number of them might be enough to make one quit…if we were alone. But we're not alone!

Whatever happens, we are called to stand firm and consider that we have been bought with a great price. We are not our own.[47] We have not

---

[46] Philippians 1:27–29
[47] 1 Corinthians 6:20

been purchased with some cheap price, like trinkets in a dollar store! God purchased the Church with His own blood.[48] Because of the great price with which we have been purchased, God's instruction to us is to:

Conduct yourselves in a manner worthy of the gospel of Christ

The phrase "conduct yourselves" deals with how we actually live out our faith. As beautiful as the Old English of the King James Version is, there are often times when the English of four hundred years ago simply does not convey the meaning of the original words written by Paul. In fact, sometimes it obscures it. Paul's instruction to the church in Philippians 1:27 is just such a verse. In the KJV it reads, "Only let your conversation be as it becometh the gospel of Christ."

I'm not entering into the argument here about which translations are or are not "inspired." That consideration is far outside the scope of this small book. But I will observe that the actions many believers have adopted almost seem to have been based upon the unfortunate word which is in the King James Bible—CONVERSATION. Far too many people, who claim to be followers of Christ, are satisfied to simply talk about unity, without actually doing anything substantive about restoring the unity our Lord calls us to walk in! Let's walk the talk!

Having participated in the annual Week of Prayer for Christian Unity which is held in Jerusalem, I can tell you that there appears to be much more talk about unity than there is walk. While I have observed that some of the clergymen involved in this effort truly have a heart for the unity of the Body of Christ, I have also run headlong into leaders who ignore repeated appeals for restoration, forgiveness, and unity. Even a Google search for the term "Jerusalem church unity week 2015" yields some 37,200,000 results. I have not read all 37 million of them, to be sure. But I can tell you one thing for certain, if the majority of those results were more walk than talk, we'd have a great deal more unity than we do in the Body.

Rev. Aaron Eime, my brother in the Lord who serves at Christ Church in Jerusalem, has wisely observed that "unity is a behavior." It is not enough to simply talk the talk, we must also walk the walk. Paul's command

---

[48] Acts 20:28

is to *conduct ourselves* in a manner worthy of the gospel of Christ. No instruction is given that we must agree about every element of doctrine. It's not "1-2-3-think-like-me!" Rather, it is a choice to walk in unity, based upon our relationship with Christ.

The word translated *worthy* is the Greek word *axios*, from which we get our word *axis*. It refers to the central axis on a balance scale, from which it derives its meaning of "suitable because it is recognized as fitting (having worth that 'matches' actual value)."[49] In other words, when we put the value that Christ paid for us on one side of the scale, we should conduct ourselves so that our lives *balance* the axis. Only when our own life is one of total devotion to the gospel, can we hope to balance it against His life of total devotion to the gospel.

Paul ties one primary element to this choice to conduct ourselves in a manner worthy of the gospel of Christ. We don't get to just wake up in the morning and say, "Well, today I want to walk worthy of the gospel," and just apply whatever measure we wish to that lofty goal. No, Paul tells us we must:

STAND FIRM IN ONE SPIRIT, CONTENDING AS ONE MAN FOR THE FAITH OF THE GOSPEL

This phrase "contending as one man" comes from two words Paul uses:' *sun* and *athleo*. We get our word *athletics* from the last word, and it carries the meaning of "compete together with others" and even to "cooperate vigorously with."[50] This is a team effort. It is not something that we can accomplish on our own. We need one another. "If the eye should say to the hand..." No, it doesn't work that way. We cannot display the fullness of God's glory without cooperating vigorously with the others in the Body.

Perhaps this may be the time to recall that Jesus said, "Where two or three gather in my name, there am I with them."[51] We don't get the option of a lonely walk with Jesus. He says it may be as small as two or three, but it is not just "Jesus and me." Jesus calls us to communion with one another, not just with Him. You may be the most gifted foot in the world, but as a

---
[49] *Strong's Exhaustive Concordance of the Bible*, Greek 516, ξίως
[50] *Strong's Exhaustive Concordance of the Bible*, Greek 4866, συναθλέω
[51] Matthew 18:20

Discerning the Body

foot, you'd make a terrible eye or ear. In order for us to be a complete Body, we require each other's presence and participation. Without one another, we can never reach the potential to which Jesus called His Church.

Paul was saying, "I just want to hear that everyone in the Church is deliberately striving together. That's when you'll be unstoppable. That's when you'll see the victory that is in Christ's glory." When you're working together as ONE, when you become the team you were created to be, the gospel will be advanced. God's glory is displayed in our unity. That's the lesson of John 17 in a nutshell.

> Jesus calls us to communion with one another, not just with Him.

We are called to stand firm in one Spirit. There is no room for a spirit of contention, a spirit of pride, or a spirit of anger. He has, instead, given us the Spirit of adoption, according to Romans 8:15. We have all been adopted into His family and are, therefore, placed into relationship with one another. We are called to contend together as one man. This is the image of unity.

Striving together…

UNSTOPPABLE!

Paul envisions the church as a family of people standing firm in one spirit, who spend their days contending as one man for the gospel of Jesus Christ, sharing the good news with an unsaved world; and then bringing the family together on the Lord's Day to support and encourage one another in the worship of Christ. This is the image of the Church that Paul is setting before the Philippians, an image of a Body that works together and loves doing it. A Body where each part recognizes its need for the other parts, knowing that no single part of the Body is sufficient to accomplish the mission Jesus has set before the Body of Christ as a whole.

When we're contending as one man for the faith of the gospel, that's when we can live our faith without being frightened *in any way* by those who oppose us. Make no mistake, when we deliberately seek to gather together in the unity as the Body of Christ contending as one man for the faith of the Gospel, there will be those who oppose us. Jesus reminds us that they hated Him first, and we can expect no less.[52] The kingdom of darkness

---
[52] John 15:8

always opposes the Kingdom of light. Even though satan is a defeated foe, he has not yet surrendered.

As such, we can expect there to be an onslaught of lies, attacks, and even persecution. The secular world will claim that proclaiming the gospel of Jesus Christ is an act of prejudice and exclusivity. They will ask questions like, "How can you possibly say you have the *only* way of truth?" as if their objections themselves offered some sort of alternative. The fact remains, we have been sent as ambassadors of Christ, and ambassadors are not allowed to choose their own message.

The message of the gospel is clear. Peter's words to the high priest and the Sanhedrin are as true today as they were when he spoke them. "Salvation is found in *no one else*, for there is no other name under heaven given to men by which we must be saved"[53] (emphasis added). Our message is not that we have the only way of truth, which would be to say that our particular method of worship or practice is the only way. Our message is that He has the only way of truth. Jesus alone offers the means for salvation!

This is not a small distinction. One may properly follow and worship Jesus in any of a vast number of traditions, languages, and expressions, but He is still the only way for us to be saved. Salvation is found in no one else. If this is not the message of the gospel, then Jesus died in vain and wasted His life. If there were another means for salvation available, the Father would have answered Jesus' prayer in the Garden of Gethsemane quite differently.

We cannot allow fear of attacks from outside the Body to stop us from sharing the message of love and grace. Jesus said He was sending us out as sheep among wolves, in reference to the proclamation of the gospel.[54] Over the next several verses the Lord paints a fairly grim picture of the attacks and persecution the Church will face. And yet, in spite of this opposition from those outside the Body, He encourages us by saying, "Do not be afraid of them."[55]

Sadly, even the call to unify the Body of Christ will face opposition

---

[53] Acts 4:12
[54] Matthew 10:16
[55] Matthew 10:26

and that from the very ones He is seeking to unify. There will be voices shouting from within the Body claiming all manner of things. Some will loudly insist that there can be no unity unless and until everyone else accepts their specific denominational point of view and adopts their mantle, as if the only path to true unity was for all of us to become Southern Baptist, or Roman Catholic, or Foursquare, or Presbyterian, or *insert-your-church-name-here*.

That is certainly not the solution.

Akin to the first argument, will be those who claim that only Luther, or Calvin, or General Booth, or *fill-in-your-favorite-leader* had the *proper* revelation of how we must all worship and serve Christ, so we should at least follow his form of worship—would that it could be so simple! Unfortunately, it is not.

There will also be those who accuse us of abandoning the faith in favor of some kumbaya moment of a Christ-less and doctrine-less ecumenism. I will speak to this in the next two chapters; first addressing the basis of salvation by grace through faith and then examining the historical stance of the Church on the matter. But these voices making charges of a faithless ecumenism must be challenged with the question, "If Jesus Himself says that a person is *in Christ*, on what basis do we dare say they are not?" Because, I remind you, we are speaking only about those who are already in Christ coming together in unity.

We cannot allow fear of attacks from inside the Body to stop us from seeking a basis of unity in the love and grace of Christ Jesus our Lord. "For God has not given us a spirit of fear and timidity, but of power, love, and self-discipline."[56] We cannot be cowards, which is the root of the word for fear which Paul uses here. Our Lord has given us a Spirit of POWER, because the task before us will require a powerful Body determined to advance the gospel. Our Lord has given us a Spirit of LOVE, because the task before us will require a great deal of acceptance, understanding, and the overlooking of both old and new injuries. Our Lord has given us a Spirit of SELF-DISCIPLINE, because the task before us will be neither quick nor easy.

One of the most important reasons for the Body of Christ to stand in unity, contending as one man for the faith of the gospel is that:

---
[56] 2 Timothy 1:7 (NLT)

THIS IS A SIGN TO THEM THAT THEY WILL BE DESTROYED, BUT THAT YOU WILL BE SAVED— AND THAT BY GOD

The very fact that we refuse to be divided in the face of the opposition that will come against the Body is a sure and certain sign to those who oppose us. Fox's Book of martyrs records the death of a man named Basilides, a Roman military officer who converted to Christianity after being ordered to attend the execution of some young Christian women. So struck was he by their unity in faith, he was compelled to accept this Christ for whom they so willingly laid down their lives. A few days later, his decision cost him his own life. The women's faith was a sign to Basilides that, without Christ, he would be destroyed and that they would be saved. But he didn't lose his life, instead, he gained it!

This is what Paul was speaking about. He was saying that if we who call ourselves by the name of Christ and stand united "as one man," then our witness of unity will compel the understanding of the truth of our gospel in those who oppose us. If we stand together in the face of anything and everything the enemy can throw at us, and if we say, "It doesn't matter who says we are crazy for believing Jesus' call to discipleship," this would be a sign to them. When we can say, "It doesn't matter if we have some differences in our practice of faith or that we prefer variant expressions of worship," this will be a sign to them that the Lord is on our side.

Once the world sees that we refuse to be divided, that our primary focus is walking in unity with our Lord and Savior, Jesus Christ, they will see this as a sign that salvation is ours. Moreover, aside from the sign that we have the salvation of the gospel of Christ, they will see that without His gospel, they will be destroyed.

This is a clear message: We need to walk in unity. Unless and until we, who are in Christ, "stand firm in one spirit, contending as one man for the faith of the gospel," we have no such sign to offer the world. History shows us that we have experienced major outpourings of revival and power when we, as believers, have focused upon the gospel and have refused to be separated by race, non-essential doctrine, or denominational practices. Some of these revivals have swept nations. But we have yet to see the entire world confronted by the message of the gospel. The sad fact is that our disunity must be seen as a major factor.

The question must be addressed. On what basis can the entire Church come together as one Body—THE Body of Christ?

Let's examine that question next.

Chapter 4

✟

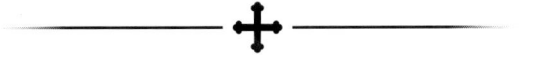

IN CHRIST

"IN ESSENTIALS UNITY,
　　IN NON-ESSENTIALS LIBERTY,
　　　　IN ALL THINGS CHARITY."

The above quote, widely (though falsely) attributed to St. Augustine of Hippo, was actually first used by the Archbishop of Split.[57] Yeah, I know, God has an amazing sense of humor. You can't make this stuff up. One of the most quoted phrases on unity came from a man whose ministry base was a place named *Split*. Not only that, but he managed to get himself branded as a heretic by both the Protestant and the Roman Catholic churches. Sounds like they had a difficult time agreeing on what the "essentials" were to establish a base of unity. No wonder people prefer to attribute that quote to one of the most respected doctors of the church.

Faulty history aside, the concept of identifying an essential base upon which the entire Church can stand united is neither a new thing nor is it an easy one. As we will see in the next chapter, it was the primary aim of one of the major post-apostolic ecumenical councils of the church. Over the ensuing years, it is a topic that has been addressed countless times, by many far more qualified than I. Learned theologians have attacked this issue and various attempts have been made. This small book is not going to be the

---

[57] de Dominis, Marco Antonio, Archbishop of Split (Spalato) (1617), "Book 4, Chapter 8," De republica ecclesiastica libri X 1, London, p. 676

venue for a detailed analysis of these efforts. I'll simply observe that, by and large, these endeavors have produced much more heat than light.

It has been said that "fools rush in where angels fear to tread," so it is on that basis that I claim my primary qualification to enter into this historic fray. I am not a theologian, though I hold a graduate degree in theology. Neither am I a historian. I do not even claim to be particularly strong in the study of church history. So let me claim my chief credential—I AM A FOOL. On that basis alone, I begin.

I am simply a man who is foolish enough to believe that the Scriptures are utterly, totally, completely, and fully inspired by the Almighty. While I make no pretense at having a total grasp even of their contents, let alone the deep meaning and application of every verse, I confess to being jealous of the original apostles. I would love to have the Lord open my mind to understand all of the Scriptures as He opened theirs.[58] In my foolishness, I see within the Scriptures a clear and unmistakable call to UNITY IN THE BODY OF CHRIST.

I am so foolish, in fact, that I believe that this is possible.

If Jesus tarries, the church will soon embark upon our third millennium. If we look at our lives and experiences as the Body of Christ, we must admit we have fallen far short of the mark set for us by our Lord in John's gospel. "I pray also for those who will believe in Me through their message, that all of them may be one, Father, just as You are in Me and I am in You. May they also be in Us so that the world may believe that You have sent Me."[59] I read those words, the impassioned prayer of the One Whom we call our Lord, and I cringe inside.

First of all, I cringe because I know that I have played a role in building walls. They've been based upon convictions dearly held, and they've often been based upon my understanding of the Scriptures. The only problem is that, over the years, my convictions and understandings have changed. I would prefer to say, they have "matured." Though that is certainly my hope, I dare not insist upon it. The real problem is that today the walls I would build are different from the walls I have built in the past. This alone gives rise to concern in me.

---

[58] Luke 24:45
[59] John 17:20–21

I invite you to take a moment now and consider your own spiritual development. If you have walked with the Lord for any significant length of time, try to recall some of the things that seemed so clear and foundational to you at first but which you now have a bit of a different perspective on.

No, really. Stop and think for a moment. Find one such idea in your own history. As you remember it, recall the process by which you came to adopt the greater understanding you now hold. Remind yourself of what the process of growth felt like. It was a bit unnerving, perhaps. Possibly it involved some conflict. But what came out of it was (hopefully) a deeper and fuller understanding of the magnitude and greatness of our God.

I'll share one such element from my life. My experience of coming to know Christ in a personal and life-changing way, which occurred in February of 1979 in an Assemblies of God church. Having grown up in the Roman Catholic Church, this new foray into evangelical pentecostalism was quite a change. Even my limited experience with charismatic Catholics had not prepared me for the changes I was about to face. But, as time went by, I grew in my understanding of the Spirit-filled life and the gifts of the Spirit.

Many years later, I taught a series of classes I had written on the topic of "The Ministry of the Holy Spirit Today" to an Assemblies of God Sunday School. In the class dealing with the Baptism of the Holy Spirit, I taught everyone that *the* initial evidence of someone receiving the Holy Spirit was the spiritual gift of speaking in tongues.

The reason I taught this was because I had approached the preparation of the class notes from the standpoint of AG doctrine. This is the position of the Assemblies of God. It was the position I held then. Let me state clearly here that I do pray in tongues, and I accept it as a valid and vibrant spiritual gift for today. Like Paul, the apostle, I wish you would all pray in tongues. However, based upon a plain reading of the Scriptures, I would have to say today that the initial evidence of someone receiving the Holy Spirit is an endowment of power to be an effective witness for the gospel of Christ, which is often accompanied by other manifestations of spiritual gifts. Speaking in other tongues may be (and often is) one of these gifts, but it is not *the* initial evidence.

My point is this, each of us can be influenced by the particular viewpoints and stances of our own denomination and church. Hopefully, that influence is positive. But all too often, we can be lulled into taking an e*isegetical* approach to learning our doctrine. Exegesis is the process of examining a text of Scripture and attempting to draw out the meaning of that text. It asks the question, "What does this text say?" Eisegesis can be described as taking the opposite approach, that of taking a doctrine or idea and applying proof texts to support the thought. The great risk with an eisegetical approach to doctrine is the danger of taking verses out of context or not considering other relevant and significant verses that deal with the issue at hand.

Taking verses out of context can be a dangerous thing. For example, I could "prove" from the Bible that suicide is a wonderful idea by beginning with Matthew 27:5, the verse that tells us Judas went and hanged himself. I could support this false idea by reminding you of Luke 10:37, where Jesus says to go and do likewise. And, finally, this absurd example could be given added urgency by recalling that the Lord Himself told Judas that what he was about to do, he should do quickly. Point proven, right?

Wrong! Absolutely wrong! Totally wrong! This approach rips the text from its context and ignores the plain teaching of other significant Scriptures on the matter. The only point I have truly proven here is that it is far too easy to be misled, if we do not consider the full teaching of Scripture on a topic, while forming our doctrinal positions.

How many of our walls have been built on foundations that are more eisegetical than exegetical, or positions that *seem to be correct* and yet fail to consider a fuller teaching of the Scriptures on any given matter?

Let's consider again the prayer of Christ in the upper room that night. He said "I pray also for those who will believe in Me through their message, that all of them may be one, Father, just as You are in Me and I am in You. May they also be in Us so that the world may believe that You have sent Me."[60]

---

[60] John 17:20–21

I PRAY ALSO FOR THOSE WHO WILL BELIEVE IN ME THROUGH THEIR MESSAGE

If you are someone who has believed and accepted the gospel of Jesus Christ, then you are one of those Jesus is speaking about in His prayer. "Their message" was the message the apostles seated around that table began proclaiming, after being filled with the Holy Spirit and empowered to deliver it. It was succinctly summed up by Peter to the Sanhedrin when he and John were on trial for preaching Jesus as the Messiah. Peter said, "Salvation is found in no one else, for there is no other name under heaven given to men by which we must be saved."[61]

The inescapable conclusion to be drawn from this verse is that Jesus was praying for each and every person who would come to believe in Him through their message. He was praying for you and me.

What was it that He sought from the Father?

THAT ALL OF THEM MAY BE ONE, FATHER

Jesus was very clear in the intent of His prayer. We who believe in Christ through the message of the apostles are the "them." And His prayer to His heavenly Father is that all of "them" may be one.

All? Yes, all.

That is a phenomenal statement coming from the Messiah. He was actually praying that *all* of us would be able to stand with one another in total unity. But achieving that level of unity has proven to be untenably difficult, several good and worthwhile efforts throughout various points in the church's history notwithstanding. Our lack of success becomes even clearer when we consider the example the Lord used to illustrate the level of unity He was praying for us to have.

FATHER, JUST AS YOU ARE IN ME AND I AM IN YOU, MAY THEY ALSO BE IN US

Really? Jesus expects us to walk in the same level of unity that He has with the Father! I don't know what you feel when you stop to consider

---
[61] Acts 4:12

the significance of His meaning. Try to look at this verse as though seeing it for the first time. It is absolutely stunning in its simplicity and its utter impossibility.

Jesus had a way of upsetting people's preconceived ideas in order to introduce a deeper understanding. One day, while preaching through the cities of Galilee, Jesus entered a synagogue on the Sabbath. One of the men worshipping inside had a shriveled hand. Jesus had just proclaimed to the Pharisees that He was the Lord of the Sabbath, now He intended to illustrate His lesson. They attempted to trap Him by asking, "Is it lawful to heal on the Sabbath?" Impossible, they thought. Their position would be unassailable. No work was permitted on the Sabbath. The doctrines and rules they had created about this were clear, specific, and detailed. And they were flawed.

> Jesus expects us to walk in the same level of unity that He has with the Father!

But Jesus was the Lord of the Sabbath, and He was about to explain how even in their intent to be righteous, they had missed a critical element. He said to them, "If any of you has a sheep and it falls into a pit on the Sabbath, will you not take hold of it and lift it out? How much more valuable is a man than a sheep! Therefore it is lawful to do good on the Sabbath."[62] His lesson is simple and direct. They had been focusing on what they shouldn't do on the Sabbath. He said it was necessary to consider also what they should do. Jesus upset their preconceived notion of what God allowed to be done on the Sabbath, in order to introduce a deeper understanding of God's love of the people for whom He created the Sabbath!

Another day He had Peter, James, and John accompany Him to the house of Jairus, the synagogue ruler whose daughter had died. Jesus had just spoken to Jairus and told him, "Don't be afraid; just believe, and she will be healed."[63] This was yet another impossible situation. (Have you noticed that Jesus never seemed to be bothered by the apparent impossibility of the things He prayed for?) When He showed up at the house and announced the girl was not dead but only asleep, the gathered mourners laughed at Him.

---
[62] Matthew 12:11–12
[63] Luke 8:50

"Oh, come on Jesus! Don't be ridiculous," they might have said. "Anybody can clearly see that she is dead! What you've just said is impossible!" Jesus was not deterred by their ridicule. Instead, He simply took the girl by the hand and gave a command—"Get up." Her spirit returned, and she obeyed. Jesus upset Jairus' preconceived notion of life, in order to introduce a deeper understanding of faith.

If I were to recount every example of Jesus walking into impossible situations and changing the anticipated outcome, this would be a very large book, indeed! But the point is this: Jesus was not concerned with the level of "possibility" or "impossibility" of what He prayed to His Father in heaven. He knows that *all things are possible* if we choose to believe in His power to act through us. To pray that His church would have the same level of unity as He and the Father have is just one more "impossible" prayer, a prayer which He intends to see fulfilled. He *must* see it fulfilled, because the outcome of our unity will be:

SO THAT THE WORLD MAY BELIEVE THAT YOU HAVE SENT ME

The Messiah is stating, in no uncertain terms, that when those of us who are in Him are able to stand in unity THEN (and, one might argue, ONLY then) will the world believe! And the world MUST believe! This is the reason Christ came to the earth. He gave His all to purchase our salvation.

If the world MUST believe, then we MUST become one! We must become one "so that the world may believe." It is really as simple as that—simple and impossible. But don't forget, Jesus isn't afraid of the impossible!

Yet the task is not impossible if Christ Himself has made the way. And, the fact is, He has done so. Could it be that the key to standing in unity has been sitting before our eyes the whole time? I am convinced that the answer to our questions on unity lies in Jesus' statement: "Just as You are in Me and I am in You. May they also be in Us."

Let's examine what it means to be "in Christ." Let's consider how this occurs, what changes take place in us when it does occur, and how that impacts our relationship with one another.

The scriptural presentation as to how one comes to know and accept

Jesus Christ as Lord and Savior is not difficult.

> If you confess with your mouth, "Jesus is Lord," and believe in your heart that God raised him from the dead, you will be saved. For it is with your heart that you believe and are justified, and it is with your mouth that you confess and are saved."[64]

Simple, direct, uncomplicated.

Earlier in his letter to the Romans, Paul made it clear that this gift was offered without consideration of who was seeking forgiveness in Christ. He wrote,

> Now a righteousness from God, apart from law, has been made known, to which the Law and the Prophets testify. This righteousness from God comes *through faith in Jesus Christ to all who believe*. There is no difference, for all have sinned and fall short of the glory of God, and are justified freely by his grace through the redemption that came by Christ Jesus.[65] (Emphasis added)

"This righteousness from God comes through faith in Jesus Christ to all who believe." It is a divine exchange of incredible magnitude. "God made Him who had no sin to be sin for us, so that in Him we might become the righteousness of God."[66] Each one of us, filthy in our sin and utterly unable to do anything about it on our own, has been invited to the divine exchange. Jesus Christ, God Himself manifest in the flesh, came and offered to take our sin upon Himself and deliver unto us His own righteousness. And, as incredible as it may seem, the offer is open to all! It is an offer apart from the law, providing justification freely by His abundant grace.

This justification is accomplished by the ministry of the Holy Spirit in our lives. Paul, after mentioning a large list of wicked actions which had characterized the members of the church in Corinth prior to their salvation, reminds them: "You were washed, you were sanctified, you were justified in

---

[64] Romans 10:9–10
[65] Romans 3:21–24
[66] 2 Corinthians 5:21

the name of the Lord Jesus Christ and by the Spirit of our God."[67]

So we clearly see that all three members of the Holy Trinity— the Father, the Son, and the Holy Spirit—chose to be involved in the process of salvation. The Father sent His Son into the world to seek and to save those who were lost. The Son voluntarily took upon Himself the penalty we should've paid for our sin and offered us His own righteousness in exchange. The Holy Spirit washed, sanctified, and justified us.

There is nothing we can do to merit this grace and nothing we can do in and of ourselves to be worthy of it. We are just another part of the "all" who have "sinned and fall short of the glory of God." Thankfully, for those who choose to believe on Him in their heart and confess Him with their mouth, we are also among the "all" who were "justified freely by his grace." Paul says it even more succinctly to the Ephesian church when he tells them: "It is by grace you have been saved, through faith—and this not from yourselves, it is the gift of God—not by works, so that no one can boast."[68]

So then, in this salvation by grace through faith, God is reconciling the world to Himself in Christ. "Therefore, if anyone is in Christ, he is a new creation; the old has gone, the new has come! All this is from God, who reconciled us to himself through Christ"[69] When we are placed *in Christ*, we become new creations! Our salvation is a creative act of the Almighty. He destroys the old and creates the new, as He places us in Christ, reconciling us to Himself. Awesome!

WE ARE SAVED BY GRACE THROUGH FAITH ALONE

On 31 October 1517, Martin Luther nailed ninety-five theses to the door of All Saints' Church in Wittenberg, Germany, in an act which has been branded as the beginning of the Protestant Revolution. One major area of dissention was the nature of salvation. For the better part of the next five centuries, the Roman Catholic and Lutheran Churches (and, for that matter, most of the Protestant denominations) have been divided upon this issue. But in recent years, issues surrounding the biblical position of salvation by grace, through faith alone, have been coming to the forefront of a number

---
[67] 1 Corinthians 6:11
[68] Ephesians 2:8–9
[69] 2 Corinthians 5:17–18

of significant discussions.

In 1974, the International Congress on World Evangelization gathered believers from more than 150 nations in Lausanne Switzerland. Renowned evangelist Billy Graham, who served as Honorary Chairman, noted that they had "invited participants from every possible nation and nearly every evangelical denomination and para-church organization in the world."[70] The invitation also included the Lutherans and the Roman Catholic Church.[71]

The members of the conference set out a five-point definition of evangelism, which included: first, the authority of the Scriptures; second, the lost-ness of man apart from Jesus Christ; third, salvation is found in Christ alone; fourth, our witness must be in both word and deed; and finally, that the evangelization of the lost, through the gospel of Jesus Christ, is completely necessary. The focus of the Church was set clearly upon the gospel, the means of salvation. *All the participants stood behind and accepted the definition.*

Twenty-five years later in October 1999, the Roman Catholic Church and the Lutheran World Federation harvested the fruit of years of discussions and signed a document known as the Joint Declaration on the Doctrine of Justification.[72] As amazing as it may seem, these two churches stated that, because they had listened to the Scriptures and gained new insights, they had come to the point where they were "now able to articulate a *common understanding* of our justification by God's grace through faith in Christ."[73]

And here is the common understanding they have both agreed to, as listed in paragraph 15.

> Together we confess: By grace alone, in faith in Christ's saving work and not because of any merit on our part, we are accepted by God and receive the Holy Spirit, who renews our hearts while equipping and calling us to good works.

Pause for a moment and re-read some of those words.

---

[70] www.lausanne.org/docs/lau1docs/0022.pdf
[71] Records of the World Congress on Evangelism, Collection 14, http://www2.wheaton.edu/bgc/archives/GUIDES/014.htm#3
[72] http://tiny.cc/JDDJ
[73] Ibid.

"By grace *alone*"—accepting a salvation based solely and exclusively upon the finished work of Christ and none of our own—deliberately agreeing that this marvelous salvation is "not because of any merit on our part." Many would have thought they'd never hear such a confession from the Roman Catholic Church. And yet, there it is! As Bishop Tony Palmer put it so succinctly, "We preach the *same gospel now*. The protest of Martin Luther is over."

Of course, this only the first step, and it is not the end of the journey. But "a journey of a thousand miles begins with a single step."[74] Let's at least rejoice in the journey that has begun. The question is whether the Church will be willing to make that journey *together* and focus more upon the needs of those who have yet to be evangelized and converted, rather than upon the differences among those of us who have.

Earlier in this book, I recounted to you the story of the inroads that are being made between the Orthodox Patriarch and the Roman Pontiff. Discussions continue as to how to advance the unity and deal with the issues that remain. What is significant is that both Patriarch Bartholomew and Pope Francis desire that these advances take place.

I also wrote about the manner in which Pope Francis reached out to evangelicals through his video message to Kenneth Copeland. As surprising as the impact of the video message was, the response of a group of key leaders of the evangelical community was even more so. The response to the video was the establishment of a new dialogue regarding the "Miracle of Unity."

That message led to a historic meeting at the Vatican between several evangelical Christian leaders and Pope Francis on June 24, 2014. The meeting was a huge success, primarily because it was done neither by might nor by strength, but by the Spirit of God. Pope Francis was astounded by the fact that the evangelical delegation represented 80 to 90 percent of the world's evangelical Christians and said, "This could ONLY be by the Holy Spirit, and we must continue to follow His leading."

The primary purpose for the meeting was to begin a dialog between Pope Francis and the evangelical Christian leaders, those who responded positively to the video message Bishop Tony had made back during his

---

[74] Lao-Tsu, Tao Te Ching, Chapter 64

January papal audience.

A secondary purpose was for the delegation to acknowledge that their protest was over. And, specifically, to discuss with Pope Francis some concrete steps forward—steps which would give all of them the occasion to publicly declare our unity. As noted earlier, that unity could be expressed and acted upon in two primary areas. The first area was an agreement on the element of FAITH: We are saved by grace and not as a result of our works. The second area was an agreement on the element of MISSION: Together we are all called to evangelize and minister the gospel of our Lord Jesus Christ.

But, as the second element of paragraph fifteen of the Joint Declaration demands, we must consider the WHOLE STORY! Because the Scriptures make it clear that, though we are saved by grace alone, we were saved for a purpose. "We are accepted by God and receive the Holy Spirit, who renews our hearts *while equipping and calling us to good works.*" Here then is the larger picture, as we see in 2 Corinthians—we are not saved BY works, but called UNTO them.

> If anyone is in Christ, he is a new creation; the old has gone, the new has come! All this is from God, who reconciled us to Himself through Christ and gave us the ministry of reconciliation: that God was reconciling the world to Himself in Christ, not counting men's sins against them. And He has committed to us the message of reconciliation. We are therefore Christ's ambassadors, as though God were making His appeal through us. We implore you on Christ's behalf: Be reconciled to God. God made Him who had no sin to be sin for us, so that in Him we might become the righteousness of God.[75]

Paul tells us that God has given us the ministry of reconciliation. Us? *Really?*

We who were dead in our trespasses and sins until He came and offered us new life? Strange as it may seem, the answer to that question is a resounding, "Yes!"

---

[75] 2 Corinthians 5:17–21

God has chosen to take the ones who have been saved by His grace through faith, and commit unto them the message of this incredible reconciliation. He has chosen to appoint us as His ambassadors and make His appeal to the world through us, inviting other sinners to be reconciled to this amazing God Who chooses to forgive our sins in so gracious a manner.

The verses in Ephesians 2, where we are told we are saved by grace through faith, continue in verse 10 as follows: "For we are God's workmanship, created in Christ Jesus to do good works, which God prepared in advance for us to do."[76] We are created in Christ to do good works. So we, who are the new creation, have been given a purpose and a calling. Please note that this calling is totally apart from the gift of salvation. It is NOT something we do that merits this gift of grace. It is something we are called to because of the gift of grace.

He has prepared these works for us to do in advance. He knew us before we knew Him, and He has created us with a purpose. Moreover, we are His workmanship, which speaks to the preparation He has worked into each one of us, the gifts He has given to us. We are, each one of us in Christ, prepared and equipped for specific works.

The image Paul makes reference to—one of an ambassador—is a significant one. An ambassador is the highest official representative that a head of state can send to another nation. He represents the full power of the one who sent him and is called to carry the message of his sovereign. The ambassador is expected to subject his personal interests to those of the one who placed him in his role, and to serve the interests of the nation or kingdom he represents above all else.

Though these responsibilities apply equally to all ambassadors, it should be immediately evident that not all ambassadors are exactly the same, even ambassadors employed by the same nation. For example, if the United Kingdom sends an ambassador to Spain to represent the Crown, he would likely be a person who is familiar with the language, customs, and social interactions of the people who live in Spain. He would perform his services differently than an ambassador who was sent to Ghana or to China. The task is not different, nor the interests, only the methods of accomplishing those tasks and the means of communicating and advancing those interests.

---

[76] Ephesians 2:10

As ambassadors for the King of Kings, we are not so very different. We are saved by grace through faith alone; unto good works.

We have arrived at the core "essential" in which we need to find unity. If we would say, "IN ESSENTIALS UNITY," then I would submit the singular essential to this unity is our foundation of being in Christ. I refer to this as the "transformational essential." This is evident from Jesus' prayer in John 17, when He said "I pray also for those who will believe in Me through their message, that *all of them* may be one, Father, just as You are in Me and I am in You. May they also be in Us so that the world may believe that you have sent me"[77] (emphasis added).

I now repeat the question I asked in an earlier chapter, because it is so critical to establish this foundation:

Isn't the final arbiter of him who is *in Christ*...well, CHRIST?

God has chosen to deliver a righteousness from God, which comes through faith in Jesus Christ to all who believe. We might not agree with His choices or may find them difficult to embrace when faced with others who have accepted His offer of salvation by grace through faith. The others He has chosen to accept in Christ may appear to be too different from us and our congregations. They may not embrace our particular method of worship. They may hold to some strange doctrines which we find difficult to accept.

But I am forced to ask, knowing the struggles I personally face in being open and understanding with some of my brothers and sisters in the Kingdom—who will be the final arbiter of who is in Christ and who is not? If Christ Himself has accepted them, if He has placed them *in Christ* by virtue of the washing, cleansing, and justification of the Holy Spirit, who am I to reject them?

There will be expressions of worship with which I am totally uncomfortable. There will be modes of dress I will not appreciate. There will be doctrinal positions (both to the left and the right of mine) that will likely cause me a great deal of personal struggle. In short, there will certainly be more to accept than I care to embrace. But if we are speaking *only* about those who are in Christ, then these issues amount to tools of the enemy intended for division.

---

[77] John 17:20–21

There will be no end to the number of things the enemy will bring to my attention in hopes of bringing me to the point where I am willing to break the unity Christ prayed for. In fact, the unity He died to create *in Him*. But I dare not. Many of these issues may be opportunities for doctrinal growth on both sides of the aisle. But if we approach them in unity, we are much more likely to come to an understanding and resolve them.

I submit that the bottom line is a simple one—if Christ Himself has accepted someone, I must do the same. Because it is He who is Lord, not me.

Simple? Totally. Easy? Not at all. But vital to the mission to which those of us who are in Christ are called.

If I am willing to accept all whom He has accepted as my brothers and sisters in Christ, it is *His* acceptance that becomes the basis of our unity. This is the beginning of seeing John 17 fulfilled in this generation.

If Jesus, Who died on the cross in their place, has accepted them, then I must.

Chapter 5

✟

HISTORICAL FOUNDATIONS

There are two major problems with history: ignoring it and being ruled by it. Both approaches can undermine the life and growth of any relationship.

It was the philosopher George Santayana who observed that those who cannot remember the past are condemned to repeat it. I would even go so far as to adapt Mark Twain's quote, regarding those who will not read, and say: Those who *will not* remember the past are no better off than those who *cannot*. If we deliberately choose to ignore the lessons of the past, we have no basis of experience other than our own, forcing us to make the same mistakes others have made before us. Without the benefit of a historical framework, we can go on forever making and re-making mistakes, which limits our ability to accomplish our goals.

The Church is not immune to this sort of ignorance. It has been jokingly observed that, for some, "church history" begins the day after they give their life to Christ. These individuals have no concept of the previous lessons learned by our predecessors in Christ, or of historical truths, which have been firmly established and agreed upon by the entire Church, or even of the heresies that have been examined and debunked.

This sort of ignorance allows for an organization like the Jehovah's Witnesses to claim to be Christian, when in fact they teach that Jesus is not one with God. It is a doctrinal error founded upon the first of the early heresies debunked by the Church, Arianism. (Arianism was refuted by the First council of Nicaea in 325 AD.) For that matter, they also teach that the Holy Spirit is not one with God but only a force, which is the heresy of *dualism*. They further teach that most people will cease to exist after death, which is the heresy of *annihilationism*.

A historical understanding of the lessons already learned by the Church would equip believers to understand these lies and debunk the deceivers on the doorstep, but we are reaping the fruit of our ignorance. This is why C.S. Lewis argued against people reading *only* modern books, because we lose the perspective of history. He wrote,

> Every age has its own outlook. It is specially good at seeing certain truths and specially liable to make certain mistakes. We all, therefore, need the books that will correct the characteristic mistakes of our own period…Not, of course, that there is any magic about the past. People were no cleverer then than they are now; they made as many mistakes as we. *But not the same mistakes.*[78] (Emphasis added)

Lewis saw the value of escaping the blindness caused by our own time. We need the perspective of history and the experience of those who have gone before us if we are to reach higher heights and build on their knowledge.

Ignoring the past can lead to devastating errors. But being dominated by the past and not being able to adopt a new course of action, which corrects previous errors, can be just as devastating a strategy. As Christians, we have the foundation of the Word of God to lead us. We also have the guidance and direction of the Holy Spirit to teach us all things and to provide the strength we need to serve Christ well. In His ministry of teaching us all things, the Holy Spirit leads us in areas of growth. The Church initially gathered in the temple in Solomon's Colonnade.[79] They eventually abandoned that practice when persecution demanded it. The apostles originally made their gospel appeals in the synagogues of the communities they came to preach in; but this practice, too, was stopped in response to the Jews.

The solution to situations such as this is neither blindly following

---

[78] From C. S. Lewis's introduction to a new translation of Athanasisus' *On the Incarnation*, which was originally written in the fourth century.
[79] Acts 5:12

the past nor ignoring it. Being able to consider and apply the lessons of the past can direct us in the present and allow us to move into the best possible future. It is in this light that I want to examine one of the key historical foundations of the Church – specifically the statement of faith which is commonly known to Christians as the Nicene Creed.

Creeds are used to give the church a baseline for orthodox or acceptable beliefs. They define what is acceptable in terms of doctrine and deal with issues that have arisen because of controversial teachings. In other words, creeds declare truths held by the entire church.

The Nicene Creed is accepted as the foundational statement of faith by the overwhelming majority of Christian denominations on the planet, including every major Protestant denomination, the Anglican Church, the Roman Catholic Church, the Greek Orthodox Church, the Oriental Orthodox Church and the Eastern Orthodox Church. It is the oldest of the creeds of the church to have come out of the Church's ecumenical councils, having been the product of the First Council of Nicaea in 325 AD, with some additions relating to the Holy Spirit made by the Second Council of Nicaea in 381. (I remind the reader that the capital "C" in "Church" in the previous sentence is deliberate, and refers to the "one, holy, catholic and apostolic Church" of which every true believer in Jesus Christ is a member, and of which His Body on Earth is comprised.)

While many different denominations, organizations, and churches have created and shared their own "statement of faith" to outline what they believe and accept as normative, and many are wonderful. The failure they all share is that *only they* accept it. Neither the entire Church, nor even the majority of the rest of the Church accepts it. This alone ought to tell us something—something significant.

Here, then, is the **NICENE CREED**:

>We believe in one God, the Father, the Almighty,
>maker of heaven and earth,
>of all that is, seen and unseen.
>
>We believe in one Lord, Jesus Christ,
>the only Son of God, eternally begotten of the Father,
>God from God, Light from Light, true God from true God,
>begotten, not made, of one Being with the Father.
>Through Him all things were made.
>
>For us and for our salvation He came down from heaven:
>by the power of the Holy Spirit He became incarnate
>from the Virgin Mary and was made man.
>
>For our sake He was crucified under Pontius Pilate;
>He suffered death and was buried.
>On the third day He rose again
>in accordance with the Scriptures;
>He ascended into heaven
>and is seated at the right hand of the Father.
>
>He will come again in glory to judge the living and the dead,
>and His kingdom will have no end.
>
>We believe in the Holy Spirit,
>the Lord, the giver of life,
>Who proceeds from the Father and the Son.
>With the Father and the Son He is worshiped and glorified.
>He has spoken through the Prophets.
>
>We believe in one, holy, catholic and apostolic Church.
>We acknowledge one baptism for the forgiveness of sins.
>We look for the resurrection of the dead,
>and the life of the world to come.

Simple. Elegant, in fact.

This is the creed the "one, holy, catholic and apostolic Church" established as its baseline for orthodoxy, that which Vincent of Lerans identified as "the truth believed everywhere, always and by all." While it would certainly be interesting (and, for some, possibly even instructive) to go phrase by phrase through the Nicene Creed and examine it tenets and teachings, that sort of exercise would most certainly be beyond the scope of this small book. This work is not intended to provide a Bible study into the basic doctrines declared in the creed.

I am, however, making the claim that if a person has accepted Jesus Christ as his Savior, then he is *ipso facto* unquestionably *within* the Body of Christ. This is the argument I presented in chapter four, regarding when, whether and how people find themselves "in Christ."

In fact, an additional and potentially stronger point can be made: If people have chosen to accept the gift of salvation Jesus offers by grace, through faith in His finished work, *and* hold to these core doctrines, then not only are they within the Body of Christ, they are *squarely within* its historical orthodox doctrinal core. This naturally presents us with an expanded version of the same question we wrestled with before.

> If Christ Himself has accepted them, if He has placed them in Christ by virtue of the washing, cleansing, and justification of the Holy Spirit; and if their doctrine places them solidly within the orthodox core of historical Christianity, *who am I to reject them?*

I recognize the danger of adding even the issue of the most widely accepted historical creed of the Church as an additional factor in this consideration, for surely the initial element of being accepted by Christ is basis enough. But I take the risk of adding the Nicene Creed in order to underscore two points.

First, if acceptance by the One Who saved us and embracing the core truths of the faith are not enough of a basis to stand in unity, *then what is?*

Is it not truly arrogant to add our own personal or denominational standards and place them above the very choice of the Messiah Himself?

Second, if the historic creed, which was the foundational instrument of Church unity, does not eliminate the fear of a wild, Christ-less ecumenism, *then what will*? The Nicene Creed is the quintessential definition of historic Christian doctrinal orthodoxy. Perhaps it will open the eyes of some and allow them to see a basis upon which the Church can move beyond our differences and learn to embrace the fullness of the Body.

The early church found itself in a similar situation not long after it had been established. We find the story related to us in the book of the Acts of the Apostles.

The setting for this crisis of identity is a couple of seaside cities on the Mediterranean coast of Israel in the early to mid-forties. The first of them is Caesarea, then the Roman capital of the region. It was also the site of one of Herod's most ambitious building projects, a magnificent harbor, a large amphitheater, an impressive aqueduct, a temple to Caesar, and spectacular city. Jaffa,[80] the other city that plays a role in our story, is a much less important town about sixty kilometers to the south. Its smaller harbor was used mainly for the local fishermen and tradesmen.

The first dozen or so years of the Church saw persecution, primarily at the hands of the Jews, and their power was limited by the Roman occupation forces. *The Way*,[81] as the early Church was known, was an entirely Jewish sect, and only Jews were accepted. That was all about to change.

According to Acts 10, the commander of one of the elements in the Roman regiment, stationed in Caesarea, was a centurion named Cornelius. He was a devout man, seeking God with many prayers and offerings. It seems that when one seeks God, God is very willing to be found. So willing was God, in fact, He actually sent an angel with some very specific (if not strange) instructions.

> Send men to Joppa to bring back a man named Simon who is called Peter. He is staying with Simon the tanner, whose house is by the sea.[82]

---
[80] This place is also called "Joppa," and corresponds to the present day city of Yafo, just south of Tel Aviv.
[81] Acts 9:2
[82] Acts 10:5–6

So Cornelius assembled two of his servants and a devout soldier, explained the angelic command, and sent them to Joppa to find Simon Peter. Perhaps the servants were intended to deliver the message and the soldier was sent to make certain Peter was in a traveling mood. Who knows? But Cornelius need not have worried. The same God, who sent an angel to visit him, had already set about preparing Peter as well.

Peter, in a Holy Spirit induced trance, saw a vision of a sheet filled with all sorts of animals being let down from heaven. The sheet "contained all kinds of four-footed animals," the Scriptures tell us, "as well as reptiles of the earth and birds of the air."[83] And therein lay the problem, because many of those creatures were not "kosher." Peter is shocked to hear a voice from heaven instructing him to kill the animals and eat them. His response is the response of good Jew. "'Surely not, Lord!' Peter replied. 'I have never eaten anything impure or unclean.'"[84] God's answer to Peter is clear and direct: "The voice spoke to him a second time, 'Do not call anything impure that God has made clean.'"[85]

God's instruction to Peter goes beyond the eating of meat and begins to usher in a new Church age that Peter couldn't possibly conceive of. "Do not call anything impure that God has made clean." I'm sure that even Peter was confused by the vision. My guess is that Peter wondered if he had truly seen what he thought he had just seen. Evidently, God wanted Peter to be quite sure, because He repeated His vision experience for Peter two additional times.

Finally, Peter was left alone on the roof, contemplating what had just happened and, of course, what it could possibly have meant. That is when the men Cornelius had sent arrived at the door. The Holy Spirit gave one final set of instructions to Peter and told him, "'Simon, three men are looking for you. So get up and go downstairs. Do not hesitate to go with them, for I have sent them.'"[86]

Three men. No big deal! Peter dealt with men all the time—*Jewish* men. These were the only type of men that Peter, still living as a faithful Jew at that time, would have had anything to do with. When Peter arrived

---
[83] Acts 10:12
[84] Acts 10:14
[85] Acts 10:15
[86] Acts 10:19–20

downstairs he was in for a bit of a shock, because the men standing before him were definitely *not* Jewish, and one of them was a Roman soldier!

If that were not enough, the soldier informed him that a Roman centurion had sent for him. Initially, I imagine this news must have been about as welcomed as getting a letter from the IRS informing one of an audit on tax returns. Thankfully, for Peter's sake, the soldier quickly relates the story of the angelic visitation and God's instruction to invite Peter to the centurion's house.

Peter may not have had a full understanding of what God was up to at that point, but an inkling of comprehension was obviously beginning to dawn on him. I know this because he did something unthinkable—he invited the trio in to the house!

I say this is "unthinkable" because for a Jew to invite a non-Jew into his home was a violation of Jewish law. Though the Talmud made certain allowances for required social or business interactions, even these left the Jew ceremonially unclean and required the Jew to go through a process of ritual cleansing. But inviting three of them in as overnight guests would be utterly out of the question!

I can only imagine the conversation that took place that evening. It, evidently, included quite a few of the Jewish believers in Joppa, since Peter decided to take six of them with him to Caesarea the next day.[87] He was probably thinking, "The law says that each matter must be established by the testimony of two or three witnesses. I'd better take double that number, because no one is going to believe this!"

The next day Cornelius's two servants, the Roman soldier, Peter and six of the brethren from Joppa departed for Caesarea. Upon his arrival, Peter was faced with several potential social challenges. First, Peter was invited into the house of the Roman centurion. It was bad enough that Peter had invited the three travelers into the home of Simon the tanner in Joppa, but for a Jew to accept any hospitality from a non-Jew was strictly forbidden. However, Peter recalled the clear instructions he received from the angelic visitor and offered no objection. Second, in a show of reverence, Cornelius fell at Peter's feet as he entered. Peter having been raised to see such displays as blasphemous, made him stand up. Finally, Peter found

---
[87] Acts 11:12

himself in front of a large gathering of Gentiles, which certainly had to be quite uncomfortable for him.

Any one of these social barriers could have provided Peter with grounds to return to Joppa without following through on his calling. He was in a strange place with strange people, who practiced even stranger customs. The Talmudic laws forbade him from being there, but there he was. It wasn't God's law that was creating these barriers. It was the honest efforts of godly men. They only wanted to do the best they could to live in a way that would be pleasing to Him. We face the same situation today, don't we? The man-made religious rules of our various denominations spell out with whom we can associate and whom we should avoid, where we can and cannot go, and what we should or should not chew, sip, or eat.

I think he was just buying time, but Peter simply said, "May I ask why you sent for me?" Cornelius shared the story of his angelic visitor, and Peter was confronted with the direct action of God opening a door for the Gentiles. An action that, in many ways, was unimaginable for Peter. Centuries of history and untold hundreds of respected religious scholars had made the rules clear—there was to be no connection between the people who God had chosen for Himself and the *goyem* (nations other than Israel). And it wasn't simply Peter's understanding. In fact, once the visit to Caesarea came to light, the entire leadership of the nascent Church would meet in the first ecumenical council to wrestle with the issue. Peter was about to cross the line; and it was a big, dark, well-defined one at that.

Cornelius finished his story by telling Peter, "So I sent for you immediately, and it was good of you to come. Now we are all here in the presence of God to listen to everything the Lord has commanded you to tell us."[88]

We can only surmise which of the Lord's words came to mind as Peter stood before this group of people, which included leaders of the hated army who had invaded his country and ruled it with an iron fist. Perhaps he remembered the night on the beach of the Sea of Galilee, when Jesus had restored him to fellowship after Peter had placed himself on the outside, denying that he even knew Jesus. Or he could have recalled another Roman Centurion who had reached out to Christ for a miracle and Jesus' response

---
[88] Acts 10:33

commending him for his great faith. Was it the Great Commission that Peter recalled? Jesus had said, "Go into *all the world* and preach the gospel," had He not? Or maybe it was the final words Peter had heard Jesus say before He was taken up to heaven, "to the ends of the earth."

By whatever process, Peter came to the right decision. "Then Peter began to speak: 'I now realize how true it is that God does not show favoritism but accepts men from every nation who fear him and do what is right.'"[89] What an inspired way to begin to share the message of the gospel of salvation! Peter did not erect barriers but assured everyone who heard him that God would accept them if their hearts were right. He shared the good news of salvation, promising that "everyone who believes in Him receives forgiveness of sins through His name."[90]

Peter was faced with a choice related to his own historical foundations. Do you remember when I said, "There are two major problems with history, ignoring it and being ruled by it"? If Peter had allowed himself to be ruled by history, the door of the Church would not have been opened to the Gentile world at that point. Thankfully, Peter had the benefit of the heavenly vision and had learned the painful lessons that came from his previous lack of obedience to Christ.

So Peter begins to preach the gospel. He tells them "Truly I understand that God shows no partiality, but in every nation anyone who fears him and does what is right is acceptable to Him."[91] He continues to recount the events in Jerusalem related to the death, burial, and resurrection of Jesus. Finally, telling those listening that "everyone who believes in Him receives forgiveness of sins through His name."[92] I seriously doubt that Peter or any of the men from Joppa could have anticipated what happened next.

> Even as Peter was saying these things, the Holy Spirit fell upon all who were listening to the message. The Jewish believers who came with Peter were amazed that the gift of the Holy Spirit had been poured out on the Gentiles, too. For they heard them speaking in other tongues and praising God.[93]

---

[89] Acts 10:34–35
[90] Acts 10:43
[91] Acts 10:34–35 (ESV)
[92] Acts 10:43 (ESV)
[93] Acts 10:44-46 (NLT)

Historical Foundations

Now they had a problem!

Half a dozen Jews from Joppa were *illegally* in the home of a Gentile. And not just any Gentile, mind you, but a leader of the despised occupying army. Peter had assured the assembled crowd that anyone (even a Roman centurion!) who believed in Jesus would be saved. All those dirty, unclean, despicable people in the house decided to repent and, as quick as you please God just filled the whole bunch with His Holy Spirit to prove that *He had accepted them*! I can almost see our six Joppan friends with their eyes focused upon big-mouthed Peter, while they think to themselves, "This is *another* fine mess you've gotten us into!"

What's a good Jewish boy to do? Peter had just stomped on centuries of history and now untold hundreds of respected religious scholars were going to be very upset with this simple fisherman. There was NO WAY these people should be allowed into the still-very-Jewish Church, at least not according the rules man had so carefully laid down.

Peter had to make a choice, because one thing was painfully evident, in spite of the history and the scholars, GOD had decided to accept these Gentiles into the Body of Christ! God was obviously unconcerned with the religious rules that had been put in place or the social barriers which had been erected. He operated in total disregard for all of the justified feelings of hatred and anger which existed between the Jews and their Gentile host.

Peter's logic is unassailable. Jesus Christ had accepted them, and it is, after all, *His Church*. So Peter simply asked, "Can anyone object to their being baptized, now that they have received the Holy Spirit just as we did?"[94]

Evidently, no one could, because "he gave orders for them to be baptized in the name of Jesus Christ."[95] (If only the congregants in Daniel Tomberlin's church had been as wise that day the young, black lad wanted to give his life to Christ.)

Unlike Las Vegas, what happens in Caesarea obviously doesn't stay in Caesarea. Acts 11 begins with the fateful words: "The news traveled fast and in no time the leaders and friends back in Jerusalem heard about it."[96] Peter was in big trouble, especially with the ceremonial holiness crowd.

---

[94] Acts 10:47 (NLT)
[95] Acts 10:47 (NLT)
[96] Acts 11:1 (MSG)

Peter was called on the carpet before the other apostles and the leaders of the Church in Jerusalem to give an account for his actions. He delivers a blow-by-blow description, and he concludes his presentation with the inspired version of the same question I have been asking you throughout this book: "If God gave to them the same gift as He gave to us also after believing in the Lord Jesus Christ, *who was I that I could stand in God's way?*"[97] Who indeed?

This was God Himself breaking down the dividing wall between Jew and Gentile. The apostle Paul described the intent of God in this when he wrote,

> For he himself is our peace, who has made the two one and has destroyed the barrier, the dividing wall of hostility, by abolishing in his flesh the law with its commandments and regulations. His purpose was to create in himself *one new man out of the two*, thus making peace, and in this one body to reconcile both of them to God through the cross, by which he put to death their hostility.[98] (Emphasis added)

Confronted with irrefutable evidence that these Gentiles had been accepted into the Body of Christ by God Himself, the leadership laid aside every single one of their concerns and determined instead to glorify God and say, "'Well then, God has granted to the Gentiles also the repentance that leads to life.'"[99]

Today we are faced with precisely the same choice as the church in Jerusalem was then. We can dress it up in some very pretty language, but the bottom line for some of us is that God has chosen to accept some people we just don't like. Not only that, but He has called us to set aside the barriers that divide us as followers of Jesus, and allow Him to create one new man.

It took less than a few hundred years for the church to re-segment itself along the lines of Jew and Gentile. The questions the Jerusalem Council wrestled with were along the lines of "How can a Gentile call himself a

---

[97] Acts 11:17 (NASB)
[98] Ephesians 2:14–16
[99] Acts 11:17 (NASB)

Christian?" It was inconceivable to them that God might allow anyone to come to the Jewish Messiah for salvation without embracing every element of the Jewish faith. As you read through the New Testament, you find Paul arguing, time after time, with the *Judaizers*, a group of early Christians who believed that new converts had to embrace every element of the Jewish faith traditions in order to follow Jesus.

By the time we come to the first major ecumenical council of the Church after the apostolic era, the situation has totally reversed itself. Now the question had become, "How can a Jew call himself a Christian?" It was inconceivable to them that God might allow anyone to come to trust Jesus for their salvation without *abandoning* every element of the Jewish faith. Issues such as whether to observe the annual festivals or keep kosher regulations became major stumbling blocks.

This same state of affairs has continued even into the modern age, with large segments of the Body of Christ questioning whether or not Messianic Jews, people who come to faith in Christ from a Jewish background, must abandon their choices of dress and diet before they can follow Jesus. Sadly, the church has continued to make an issue of these and other non-essential elements, re-building the dividing wall of hostility, which the Lord Himself went to such great care to break down.

Paul, himself a classically trained rabbi in the school of Gamaliel, one of the most respected of the Jewish sages, told us in the book of Romans how foolish it is to allow ourselves to become divided by this sort of issue. He wrote:

> One man considers one day more sacred than another; another man considers every day alike. Each one should be fully convinced in his own mind. He who regards one day as special, does so to the Lord. He who eats meat, eats to the Lord, for he gives thanks to God; and he who abstains, does so to the Lord and gives thanks to God. For none of us lives to himself alone and none of us dies to himself alone. If we live, we live to the Lord; and if we die, we die to the Lord. So, whether we live or die, we belong to the Lord. For this very reason, Christ died

and returned to life so that he might be the Lord of both the dead and the living. You, then, why do you judge your brother? Or why do you look down on your brother? For we will all stand before God's judgment seat.[100]

Paul insisted that we stop passing judgment on one another. And he did so because none of these things is more important than the unity we are to express in Christ as we demonstrate a deep, active, and visible love for one another. What we choose to eat, how we prefer to dress, and which holidays we choose to celebrate are not the central focus of our relationship with Jesus. They never have been. Instead, we are to "make every effort to do what leads to peace and to mutual edification."[101]

Of course you'll have your preferences. So will I. We are different from one another, and our differences will express themselves in many ways. But however they are expressed, they should never be allowed to divide people who are in Christ.

We can choose to separate over a particular element of doctrine we don't like. We can determine to dismiss people because we don't like the way they dress up for church (or refuse to dress up for church). We can exclude them because we don't like where they've come from or perhaps even the color of their skin. If we do so, then we are walking in disobedience to His direct command.

Wouldn't it make much more sense if we took the biblical approach and chose to ask ourselves, "If God has accepted them after believing in the Lord Jesus Christ…

…who am I to stand in God's way?"

---

[100] Romans 14:5–10
[101] Romans 14:19

Chapter 6

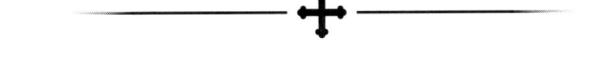

UNITY—NOT UNIFORMITY

If you believe you're familiar with the money system in the United States, I'd like you to challenge you to a little experiment.

Close your eyes for a moment and—beginning at one dollar—think through every denomination of US currency presently in use, and try to recall the name of the person featured on it. Once you've tried it on your own, have a look at the end of this chapter to see the answer. Go ahead, do it now.

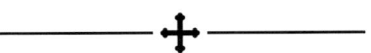

Okay, so how well did you do? I told you on the answer page that you quite likely missed at least two out of eight items and so only got 75 percent on this little quiz. If you convert that to a letter grade, that's a low C; just barely a passing grade. And I'm only speaking about remembering the currency itself, not even about whose image is on the currency!

The first miss for most of you will have been the Susan B. Anthony one dollar coin. The reason is a simple and straightforward one. When asked about currency, most people tend to think only of paper money, not coin. But, as the Merriam-Webster Dictionary has been kind enough to demonstrate, that is simply not the case. Even the Oxford English Dictionary, purported to be the most widely-accepted authority on the English language in the world, defines the word simply as a "system of money."[102]

The second typical "miss" is the two dollar bill, featuring President Thomas Jefferson. Even though there are over a billion of them in

---

[102] See http://en.oxforddictionaries.com/defination/currency

circulation, two dollar bills are so seldom used that some people refuse to accept them in payment and others have even been arrested for using them. (The most egregious case I know of is when Mike Bolesta from Baltimore was arrested, and then locked with handcuffs and leg irons to a pole in the local jail. He was held for over three hours until U.S. Secret Service Agent Leigh Turner arrived and convinced the Baltimore Police that the bills were in fact genuine US currency.)[103]

What's almost as insightful are the excuses Americans I tested this theory on gave for not knowing their own money. "Oh come on, I never deal with those silly dollar coins! I hate the way change just bounces around my pocket."

I see. So your argument is that legal tender is not valid because *you* don't use it. Have I got that right?

Here's another one: "A two dollar bill? I've never even *seen* a two dollar bill before. How am I supposed to know about those?"

Wait, what? Now we are throwing away money because you've never been exposed to it in your general experience. Really?

This approach denies the intrinsic value of the currency based upon a personal lack of knowledge or experience. I'm tempted to ask if you use hundred dollar bills very much, because if you've got a pile of those hanging around that you don't typically carry, I wouldn't mind taking them off your hands!

Well, my rebuttals above have obviously been in jest, but let's turn the corner and examine a more serious point. Many Christians are willing to score a lot less than a low-C when it comes to identifying who is and who is not part of the Body of Christ (and, oddly enough, for many of the same reasons).

"Oh come on, I never deal with those silly Charismatics! I hate the way they just swing from the chandeliers of their churches."

Really? Putting aside the fact that I've never even seen a chandelier in a charismatic church (and I've been in plenty of them all over the world), let alone having seen a congregant swinging from one, can it be that some of us are so ready to let our personal preferences marginalize (or worse,

---

[103] Search for Mike Bolesta's name on any major search engine and you'll find the Baltimore Sun article reporting upon his arrest.

eliminate) the one in four Christians around the world who, according to the Pew Research Center's Forum on Religion & Public Life, are pentecostal or charismatic believers in Jesus Christ?[104] If so, then just like that, we're scoring a low-C again and leaving only 75 percent of the Church inside what *we* will accept as Christianity.

"I've never even seen a convergence congregation that embraced liturgy and combined it with real spiritual vitality."

And *whack!* We lop off another sizeable group of people from the list of who *we* are willing to accept into Christianity. And on and on it goes. One denomination refuses to pray with another. One Christian community snubs another and will not welcome them to their worship service or, worse yet, to have communion at their table. One church says they are not about to accept someone who has truly been saved by grace through faith in Jesus Christ because he doesn't read from their approved version of the Holy Bible, which, of course, they see as the *only* true translation. If it were not so sad, it might actually be funny.

Consider for a moment the words of the hymn so often sung by George Beverly Shea during Billy Graham's altar calls:

> Just as I am, without one plea,
> But that Thy blood was shed for me,
> And that Thou bidst me come to Thee,
> O Lamb of God, I come, I come.
>
> Just as I am, Thou wilt receive,
> Wilt welcome, pardon, cleanse, relieve;
> Because Thy promise I believe,
> O Lamb of God, I come, I come.

What are your personal convictions about the claims of this hymn? Do you believe that Jesus actually *does* welcome, pardon, cleanse, and relieve *all* who come to Him? Is His invitation truly open to all? If John 3:16 is true, then "whoever" really means *whoever*.

---

[104] Read more at http://www.christianpost.com/news/more-than-1-in-4-christians-are-pentecostal-charismatic-65358/#veiUG52Xr3vPVzGt.99

Of course Christ's invitation is extended to all. So why do we act as though it is not?

The question posed by the apostle Peter remains unanswered in the Church of today—"If God gave to them the same gift as He gave to us also after believing in the Lord Jesus Christ, who was I that I could stand in God's way?"[105]

When we establish our practices, our experience, or our comfort level as the litmus test for who gets to be considered a Christian, everyone ends up with a different outcome. That is the logic that has led to a world with over 33,000 different Christian denominations, movements, communions, fellowships, and assemblies, many of which refuse to recognize the others as genuinely Christian. That's absurd on the face of it.

To overcome this preposterous logic, we must come to understand that those whom Jesus has accepted into the faith are, by definition, *in* the Body of Christ. Can we not agree to recognize that the sole factor determining who is a Christian and who is not is whether or not they have placed their faith in Jesus Christ alone for their salvation. "For it is by grace you have been saved, through faith—and this is not from yourselves, it is the gift of God."[106]

> The sole factor determining who is a Christian and who is not is whether or not they have placed their faith in Jesus Christ alone for their salvation.

We may be uncomfortable with how another believer chooses to express their worship of Jesus. But the issue is not our comfort; the issue is Christ's offer of salvation and each individual's response. Jesus Christ is the sole and exclusive arbiter of who gets to be a Christian. Once He has accepted them into His Body, they *are* Christians. Period.

If Jesus says "Yes, they are Christians!" and I say "No, they are not!" guess which one of us is correct?

Yeah, not really a tough question, is it?

It's not a tough question except when we try to put acceptance into

---

[105] Acts 11:17 (NASB)
[106] Ephesians 2:8

practice, that is. The faith that matters is not the faith we profess but the faith we practice. Because that's when we start to get focused on "how I practice my faith," as opposed to "how *you* practice your faith." In the realm of worshipping the Almighty, we tend to behave as though the way *we* choose to worship is the right way. And once we start making non-essential choices about worship (a measure of who is right and who is wrong), we end up dividing along bizarre lines.

Yet once we accept the fact that the body has different parts, it only makes sense that they would operate differently. Nobody expects a foot to work like an ear. We know they're different, and so we capitalize upon and utilize the differences. We use our ears to listen with and our feet to walk upon. We don't ask one to change and become like the other and call it unity!

Our diversity is designed into our bodies, with each part performing its own function. Scripture makes it clear that diversity has been designed into the Body of Christ. "For even as the body is one and yet has many members, and all the members of the body, though they are many, are one body, so also is Christ."[107] All the members of the body are "many." We are *deliberately different* from one another. We have different strengths and weaknesses. And because of that, we can reach different people and touch divergent areas of this planet with the gospel of Jesus Christ.

Some of our differences are because of global divergence. A church that gathers for worship in Nigeria will have a very different look and feel than a church in Nebraska, even if they are both Baptist churches, and even if they are both speaking English. The elements of our background, culture, and environment are always going to have an impact on how we communicate. When we mix those diversities, confusion and discord can result if we are not careful, (although, occasionally, the result is more hilarity than anything else).

I recall arriving in South Africa, some time ago, for a time of preaching and speaking. At that particular point in my ministry, I had not traveled very extensively. Though I was somewhat nervous, I comforted myself that this particular trip shouldn't be too difficult, because I was traveling to a nation that spoke English. What I didn't realize at that moment was that *I didn't*

---

[107] 1 Corinthians 12:12 (NASB)

speak English...I only spoke American!

The first clue that I was a stranger in a strange land, and that I was in for a very different experience than the one I had been anticipating, was the way the 8-year-old son of my host greeted me as I stepped into the baggage claim area at the Johannesburg airport.

"Hullo, Uncle! Did you bring your costume?"

My brain was deluged with a wave of confusing thoughts. The first one was, "I'm not his uncle; I don't even know this kid!" That thought was quickly followed by, "What costume?! Or, more to the point, what *is* a costume?" I was standing there in an English-speaking nation and had no idea whatsoever how to reply to a simple question from a small child. Not the best of beginnings for the arriving international speaker, let me tell you.

My brain kicked in with a piece of information that I had learned from my exposure to the Chinese culture. In China, "Uncle" was a general term of respect given to anyone significantly older. I figured that would do for now, but I still had no idea what to do with "costume." When in doubt—ask. Dropping down on one knee and placing a hand on his shoulder, I asked, "Which costume is that?"

"You know, Uncle, your *swimming* costume! We have a lovely pool at the house."

Mystery solved (or, at least, that mystery). Over the course of that trip, I was introduced to more new applications of words than I can remember. But one thing became painfully obvious. No matter how strongly I would have insisted on my fluency prior to landing in South Africa, I still didn't speak "English."

The thoroughly embarrassing part of this lesson came during one particular church service at which I spoke. Just before I was to deliver my message, the pastor slipped me a note asking me to remind the congregation that a reception had been planned for after the service. So, after I had ascended the steps and had taken my position behind the pulpit, I invited everyone to join us after the service, announcing we'd be having cookies and coffee in the foyer.

All across the church people erupted in laughter and looked strangely at one another. The pastor rushed to the pulpit, grabbed the microphone and said, "No, no, no, we'll be having BISCUITS and coffee." I was, of course, quite puzzled. Thankfully, it wasn't until after I had delivered my message that the pastor informed me that in South Africa "having cookies" is a slang term for sexual intercourse!

No wonder the church reacted the way they did! But everyone understood that my poor choice of words was a function of location ignorance, not a deliberate attempt to insult them. In other words, they could see that I didn't speak "English."

Wouldn't it be wonderful if we could learn to extend the same grace to our brothers and sisters in different parts of the world? Why do we send a missionary to a foreign land to preach the gospel to people with a rich historical culture and then insist that those who receive Christ adopt our customs, language, and modalities of worship? I have met people in Africa who were required to change their names from Abasi or Kafil to "Christian" names, like John or Paul, before they could be baptized. That's absolutely absurd! Where did the missionaries find that requirement in the Scriptures? Forget about English, let's speak "gospel!"

So let me ask, how about you? Do YOU speak gospel? Or do you perhaps only speak Southern Baptist, or Roman Catholic, or Church of God in Christ?

Some differences are just a matter of personal choice. Consider the matter of whether or not a man should wear a suit to church. In a particular church in the United States where I frequently worship, the lead pastor always wears a suit on Sunday morning. I'm sure he'd feel almost undressed if he did otherwise. A businessman who attends this church never wears his suit to a Sunday morning service, because he sees the suit as an element of formality and his relationship with Jesus as one of familiarity. I've observed other men in the congregation wear a suit to church, but from the look of it, I'm fairly certain they never wear one during the week. Bottom line: Who cares?

The point is, whether or not one chooses to wear a suit, it is a matter of personal choice and style. It is not a matter of obedience to the Holy Scriptures. (Even as I write this, I'm confident I'll get an email from someone who simply cannot believe that I would advocate *not* wearing a suit to a Sunday morning service!) In your congregation it may be the norm for all of the gentlemen to wear suits. Or you may attend a church that would be shocked to see the pastor show up in one. But either way, why on Earth would we let a matter of dress divide us?

Whether the pastor wears a clerical collar or blue jeans and t-shirt, we have no excuse for building a wall and dividing ourselves from one another. Some denominations and some cultures would find it quite strange not to have their clergy in a religious collar of some sort, while some others would find even the word "clergy" itself to be unusual. In the church I referred to earlier, if I were to show up in my clerical collar 99.9 percent of the people would be shocked. In other churches I attend regularly, if I showed up wearing anything other than my purple clerical shirt, white collar, and large pectoral cross, I would get raised eyebrows.

Let's come back to language issues. You might hear someone say, "They're not clergy. They are just our pastoral team." Or perhaps someone speaks about their *priest* instead of their *pastor,* and on and on the differences in terminology flow. But do they have to divide us, or can we simply choose to speak "gospel" and come to an agreement on the key elements of just who is and who is not in Christ?

Here is the foundational issue, from the perspective of the gospel of Jesus Christ: If anyone is in Christ, he is a new creation; the old has gone, the new has come![108] Like it or not, if you are in Christ and I am in Christ, we are connected. We are part of the *one Body*. More to the point, neither one of us gets to decide whether the other is in Christ. Only Jesus Himself gets to determine that. And Jesus has clearly laid out the means by which He makes that determination.

> If you confess with your mouth, "Jesus is Lord," and believe in your heart that God raised him from the dead, you will be saved. For it is with your heart that you believe and are justified, and it is with your mouth that you confess and are saved.[109]

Even worse than that, from the perspective of those who would prefer

---

[108] 2 Corinthians 5:17
[109] Romans 10:9–10

to limit admission to the Body, is that Paul didn't stop there. He went on to tell us in verse 13 that "Everyone who calls on the name of the Lord will be saved." Yup, everyone! Shocking, isn't it? It's called grace!

Jesus has made it clear that, though we are different members, we are all one Body. He Himself establishes the Body and craves our unity, without any intent for us to have uniformity.

I'll close this chapter recounting a significant event that occurred during my consecration as a bishop in 2012. As I have mentioned previously, I have the privilege of spending a large part of the year working in Israel, most often staying in the city of Jerusalem. Four archbishops from the Communion of Evangelical Episcopal Churches had come to Israel to spend ten days touring the land. One of the reasons they were in Israel was to confer my consecration to the episcopacy.

Among the various responsibilities I had to handle was the need to arrange a place at which the consecration could occur. One of the requirements was that it should occur in a neutral site, as our communion did not have its own church in Jerusalem at that time. (Establishing a church in Jerusalem is no small feat, let me assure you.) So I approached a good friend of mine who was the director of the Garden Tomb at the time. Not wanting to place undue pressure on him because of our relationship, I did not share that it was to be me who would be consecrated a bishop.

"Richard," I began, "Four archbishops from our communion need a place to consecrate a bishop next Sunday, and I was wondering if we could hold the service in the Garden Tomb?" Richard readily agreed, even though the Garden Tomb is typically closed on Sundays. He made arrangements for one of his assistants to be there and open the facility for us, since he was going to be away in the Galilee area during that weekend. And so Sunday morning found me preparing for the service by laying out the various vestments and accoutrements that would be given to me as part of my episcopal consecration.

As is the custom for liturgical ordinations and consecrations, I began the service dressed solely in an *alb*, which is a long white garment that symbolizes our being clothed in the purity of God's righteousness. A plain white rope called a *cincture* was tied around my waist, the mark of a slave in the early days of the Church and signifying I was a slave of Christ. From my personal perspective, this level of vesture was not too bad. Though I had spent over thirty years in the Assemblies of God, an organization that most certainly is *not* given to the use of liturgical vestments, I wasn't overly bothered by the ones I found myself wearing. That was about to change!

After a time of reading several passages related to the responsibility and calling of elders and bishops from the Scriptures, we came to the point in the service for my consecration. As the archbishops gathered around me, laid their hands upon me, and began to pray the prayer of consecration, I became keenly aware of how insignificant a man was being entrusted with so a massive responsibility.

Then, after the prayers had concluded, came the time for me to be vested as a bishop in the Church. I was handed a Bible and ordered to use it as the foundation of my leadership and teaching. Then a *stole* was draped across my shoulders, signifying the priesthood to which my faithfulness was avowed. Then a *chasuble* was placed, an outer garment signifying the royal calling to which I had entered. After that, a large cross was hung around my neck, the sign of the bishop. Next came a *miter*, the pointed hat whose shape was intended to recall the tongues of fire which had rested upon the heads of the apostles in the upper room, to remind me of the necessity of the constant infilling of the Holy Spirit. Afterwards, a ring was placed upon my right hand, symbolizing the authority of a royal signet, the authority to represent the King of Kings. And finally, a staff was placed in my left hand, reminding me that the key to this call was to feed and care for the sheep of the Good Shepherd, to Whom I was only an under shepherd.

As I stood there, fully vested as a bishop for the first time in my life, you can only imagine the weight of responsibility I felt. But there was more. I was not just aware of the weight of some newly-conferred spiritual responsibility. When I considered all that I had been vested in, I felt very, very uncomfortable; much like someone who's just been dressed in a formal coat and tails.

But then, thanks to the generosity of my friend, the time had come for me to enjoy a privilege few have had. The gate, which typically closes off the burial section of the Garden Tomb, had been opened. I was invited to enter the tomb itself for a time of private prayer.

I walked in, knelt down beside one of the two places in Jerusalem where Jesus' body is likely to have been laid, and I gathered my thoughts for prayer. I know that kneeling in that holy place, minutes after being consecrated as a bishop, I should have been able to pray some deep, holy, powerful prayer. But, I must confess, I found myself distracted by all of these various items I now wore. This former Assemblies of God preacher was most certainly out of his element!

"God," I began, "There's no sense in me pretending to fool you here. I am really uncomfortable dressed like this."

Immediately, I sensed the answer of the Lord in my spirit. His words had a sharp tone to them, almost a bit harsh. He said, "Son, I ORDAINED the robes of the high priest for MY HONOR AND GLORY, and I am *not* concerned with your comfort!"

I realized instantly what He was saying. It wasn't about me, or my experience, or my preferences, or what I had become comfortable with or accustomed to. It was about HIM—His Word, His gift of grace, His call, His majesty, and His righteousness. It is all about Him and ONLY about Him.

If we are indeed in Christ, that's the place we *all* need to come to. It is not about our comfort, our style of worship, or our preference for how our leaders should or should not dress. It is solely, ultimately, and exclusively about Him and Him alone.

It is about His gift to us and His prayer for us. He knows we are different. He created us that way. Still His prayer for us is that *we will be one*!

Who are we to stand in His way?

The Currency Question Answered

In the beginning of chapter six, I asked you to close your eyes for a moment and, beginning at one dollar, to think through every denomination of US currency and try to recall who is featured on the note.

The Merriam-Webster Dictionary provides the following definition of the word *currency:* "The money that a country uses." It goes on to further clarify the definition by stating, "Something (as coins, treasury notes, and banknotes) that is in circulation as a medium of exchange."[110]

Why would I bother to explain the definition of the word currency, you may wonder? Well, the reason should become clear as you read the below list. I develop my point a bit more in the chapter, but the bottom line is that you most likely missed the Anthony one dollar coin. Also, it is probable that you skipped the two dollar bill.

Here is the correct answer, as of the publishing of this book.

1. Susan B. Anthony – ONE DOLLAR
2. George Washington – ONE DOLLAR
3. Thomas Jefferson – TWO DOLLARS
4. Abraham Lincoln – FIVE DOLLARS
5. Alexander Hamilton – TEN DOLLARS
6. Andrew Jackson – TWENTY DOLLARS
7. Ulysses S. Grant – FIFTY DOLLARS
8. Benjamin Franklin – ONE HUNDRED DOLLARS

---
110 See http://www.merriam-webster.com/dictionary/currency

Chapter 7

UNITY—NOT UNIFICATION

In one form or another and to varying degrees of focus, Christian worship has always included singing songs of praise and adoration, reading from the Scriptures, praying, and sharing in the Lord's Table. In most of our faith traditions, it still does.

To be sure, some churches may celebrate the Lord's Table every week, while others only do so once a month or only during an Easter week service. Some of the Body's faith communities invest a great deal of time, talent, and treasure in the music that will go into a worship service at their church, while other congregations totally avoid the use of any musical instruments at all in their services. But these, or any number of other distinctions we could discuss, need not divide us. They represent choices of expression, but they do not represent the absolutes of faith. We can, indeed, we *must*, agree to stand on the core elements of the faith, as we have already discussed.

In coming to the unity in the Body of Christ, which Jesus prayed for in John 17, the goal is most certainly *not* to change the character of our individual congregations and make everyone worship in the same way. No one is suggesting the establishment of the Foursquare EpiscoBapterian Luthigistic Evangematic Southern Apostolic Presbiholiness Conservative Romagational Orthocostal Bible Community of Prophecy and Catholic Power in Christ Church. (My apologies if I missed your favorite flavor.)

The true goal of our worship services is to glorify the One who sacrificed His life to save us, to encourage biblically-based worship in a relevant expression capable of reaching local people with the message of the gospel and drawing them in to a love-affair with Jesus Christ. This, out of necessity, will require diversity in our expressions, even within the same community. That is why we are a body.

Let's attack the elephant in the room head on. The great fear of the end times is the establishment of one world religion. Any time someone begins to talk about unity in the Body of Christ and actually *does* something about it, we begin to hear the warning cries about the Antichrist. It never takes too long before someone quotes Revelation 13:12, warning that the second beast will make "the earth and those who dwell in it to worship the first beast"[111] Everyone—great and small—will be forced to abandon all other worship and required to worship the satanic first beast.

Of course, we cannot ignore the warnings of Scripture in this regard. But neither can we blindly apply them where they absolutely do not fit. It must be realized that satan always attempts to pervert the righteous and holy things God has ordained. He always deceives. He uses force to advance his evil plan, whereas God Almighty uses only love to draw us to His holy plan. Our spiritual enemy intends our destruction.

Jesus warned us that "The thief does not come except to steal, and to kill, and to destroy. I have come that they may have life, and that they may have it more abundantly."[112] Satan promises abundance, while actually stealing everything he promises. Christ delivers the life He promises, the very life He purchased for us with His own blood, and He delivers it in abundance!

So let's examine the claim and see if the great fear of the end times—the establishment of one Christ-less world religion—can possibly be the same thing Jesus Christ prayed for in John 17. Can the willing unity of His Body, in accordance with the very prayer of Jesus Himself conceivably be the same as the forced unity of everyone on the planet, brought about by the lies of the enemy?

The answer, of course, is a resounding, "No!"

To take the unity of believers in Jesus, in the love and grace of Christ for which our Savior prayed in John 17, and equate it with the diabolic deception described in Revelation 13 is in and of itself playing into the confusion of the enemy. These two things could not possibly be more

---

[111] Rev 13:12 (NASB)
[112] John 10:10 (NKJV)

different from one another, even if the *only* thing you examine is the source: one is Christ Himself and the other is satan.

The all-important question then becomes, "How can I know for certain what the difference is?" Here's how. Determine whether the object of worship is the authentic Jesus presented in the Gospels, not just some made-up Christ, formed in the image and understanding of someone's whims. Not a powerless and unbiblical caricature of the true Jesus.

To know if the Jesus being worshiped (in unity) is *truly* the One Lord, you need to know if the worship is being directed toward Jesus Christ, the only Son of God, eternally begotten of the Father, the One Who is God from God, Light from Light, true God from true God, begotten, not made, of One being with the Father. You need to see that it is the same Jesus, through whom all things were made.

The object of our worship must be the very Jesus Who, for us and for our salvation, came down from heaven by the power of the Holy Spirit, became incarnate from the Virgin Mary and was made man. The true Jesus who, for our sake, was crucified under Pontius Pilate, suffered death and was buried, and rose again on the third day, in accordance with the Scriptures.

You must know if we're talking about the Jesus Who ascended into heaven and is seated at the right hand of the Father. The same One Who will come again in glory, to judge the living and the dead, the very One Whose Kingdom will have no end.

———— ✠ ————

If THAT Jesus is the one calling us to unity as believers, if it is the message of THAT Messiah we come together to preach to a lost and dying world, then there is *only one voice* who would call that a diabolic deception, and that is the voice of the great deceiver himself.

———

You cannot bypass the fact that Jesus is calling His Body to unity. This is explicit in the several Scriptures we have examined throughout this book. The one who calls Jesus' motivation for this "satanic," then stands condemned by the words of Jesus Himself.

Allow me to point out that someone who would make this accusation against Jesus today would be standing perilously close to the same ground occupied by the scribes of two millennia ago, the very teachers of the law, which we read about in Mark 3. They accused Jesus of being possessed by satan. "And the teachers of the law who came down from Jerusalem said, 'He is possessed by Beelzebul! By the prince of demons he is driving out demons.'"[113]

Jesus' answer to these accusers is as valid today as it was the moment He spoke it.

> So Jesus called them over to him and began to speak to them in parables: "How can satan drive out satan? If a kingdom is divided against itself, that kingdom cannot stand. If a house is divided against itself, that house cannot stand. And if satan opposes himself and is divided, he cannot stand; his end has come."[114]

It *cannot* be both Jesus and satan who are calling the true, blood-washed Body of Christ into a unity that will display the glory of God to a lost and dying world. We know the prayer of the Messiah for those gathered in the upper room, and for those who would believe in Him because of the witness of the apostles, the prayer was for all of them to be *one*, as He and His Father are one. This was the heart-felt cry of the One Who was about to give His life as a ransom for many. His own lips tied the three concepts of our unity, the display of the glory of God, and the salvation of the world together.

It cannot be satan who calls the Church to fulfill her mission and preach the gospel to the ends of the earth. It is impossible for satan to drive out satan! The problem is not that those who join Jesus in praying for the unity of His Body are being deceived by the enemy. The problem is that, for centuries, we have allowed ourselves to become divided. One only need look around to see the powerlessness prophesied by Jesus coming to pass

---
[113] Mark 3:22
[114] Mark 3:23-25

in our own lives. Jesus was totally correct: A house divided against itself cannot stand!

The powerlessness of the Church to stem the tide of evil the enemy is mounting in his determination to destroy this planet and its inhabitants finds its foundation in our lack of unity. We compound it by our prayerlessness. We magnify it by our refusal to obey Him and His Word. We enlarge the impact of our powerlessness by our determined and deliberate disobedience. Our Lord has warned us, "If a kingdom is divided against itself, that kingdom cannot stand." Yet we insist that we know better than Him and start another denomination every other day, just to prove we're right.

As if that were not bad enough, when the call goes forth to abandon our petty differences within the Body of Christ and come together "endeavoring to (forge) the unity of the Spirit in the bond of peace,"[115] some religious voice is sure to raise the cry that this is establishing a "one world order."

The lie against unity never changes. But, then again, why should it? It has continued to work every time satan puts it forth. To take the goal of obedience in one of the final prayers of Jesus and assign satanic sources to it is blasphemy. As I read them, the next verses in Mark's gospel are frighteningly clear.

> Truly I tell you, people can be forgiven all their sins and every slander they utter, but whoever blasphemes against the Holy Spirit will never be forgiven; they are guilty of an eternal sin. He said this because they were saying, "He has an impure spirit."[116]

The scribes were assigning satanic motives to the message of salvation Jesus was preaching. Jesus' warning is blunt, declaring that those who blaspheme the Holy Spirit, by attributing satanic influence to Christ's proclamation, risk eternal damnation.

The gospel that a unified Church preaches and the obedience demanded by the beasts of Revelation are totally and absolutely different! There is simply no comparison between them. The false worship commanded by the

---

[115] Ephesians 4:3 (NKJV). But note that I had to replace the word "keep" with the word "forge", because we cannot keep what we do not currently possess.
[116] Mark 3:28-30

beast is not only a far cry from the worship of Jesus Christ (about which we are speaking), it is actually the diametric opposite of it.

Take a look at the table below and see the comparison side by side.

TRUE GOSPEL	FALSE GOSPEL
Jesus *invites* His Church to unify around His message	Satan *forces* the entire world to be unified around his message
Jesus is the *truth* and leads us in all truth	Satan is a *liar,* and deceives all who follow him
Jesus displayed His power by rising from the dead	Satan displays his power by the false signs he performs
Jesus invites a love response, which is freely given	Satan demands a forced, commanded response
The ultimate goal of the True Gospel is the worship of the one true God	The ultimate goal of the False Gospel is to deprive the one true God of the worship He is due

Jesus has prayed for His entire Body to be one, just as He and His Heavenly Father are one. In the two thousand years since He prayed that prayer, He has never once *forced* His Body to be unified. The reason for this is also simple—love is *always* a choice. Jesus, more than anyone, knows that love cannot be forced upon someone; love cannot be commanded or coerced. It must be given freely and offered in its totality. This is the highest expression of love—the only true expression.

The reason the satanic beast forces all who dwell on the earth into a single world religion is a very simple one, satan's goal has always been to steal the worship due the Almighty God. He lies, he steals, and he kills.

He promised the world power and control. Yet, when the world responds, the enemy ends up with the power and the world ends up with the pain. It is Genesis 3 repeated over and over again, in cities and nations around the globe. That is the goal of the enemy's one world order.

But if we are talking about the Jesus who is described and clearly articulated in the Nicene Creed, then we are talking about worshipping the One true God. Anything less and we've lost the focus of Whom we are supposed to be worshipping. And it is the worship of the one true God by the one true Church, living in unity and walking in love, which will display the glory of that one true God to a lost and dying world, which has been deceived by the father of lies.

Who is that ONE TRUE CHURCH? As has been said repeatedly throughout this book, it is none other than *everyone* who has accepted Jesus Christ as their Lord and Savior, who has been made a new creation by the power of the Almighty God. All those who have been washed in the blood of the Lamb, everyone who has been sanctified by the sealing of the Holy Spirit, the totality of everyone who has been justified in the name of the Lord Jesus Christ and by the Spirit of our God.[117] Anyone and everyone who can rightfully make that claim, in truth, is part of the ONE TRUE CHURCH, the Church that Jesus Christ came to Earth for and established by His life, death, resurrection, and ascension into heaven.

This is the Church that He is coming back to reclaim. This is His beloved bride. And, make no mistake, His Church is *His*, because it belongs to Him. The Church is relational, not institutional! His Church is made up of those who are in Christ—all of them. Those who are in Christ are a body, made up of different parts; designed for diversity, not uniformity. Our diversity is intended to be expressed in unity so that we can proclaim the message of the love of Christ to a lost and dying world.

We live in a generation equipped with tools and technology no generation before us has had. We possess capabilities that were the lore of science fiction two short decades ago. Unfortunately, the problem is not our technological capacity. It is our stubborn insistence that *our* particular flavor of Christianity is the only way to serve Him. It's an insistence that is preventing the message of the gospel from reaching a lost and dying world.

---
[117] See 1 Corinthians 6:11

When will we open our eyes to the clear teaching of the New Testament and see that we are a Body? No one is suggesting you abandon your personal choice of worship style so that we can all be exactly the same. But we must be willing to lift up our eyes and see that the fields are white for harvest, and *all of us* in the Body of Christ are called to labor TOGETHER to harvest them.

The Church *is* relational, not institutional! His Church is made up of ALL those who are in Christ, whether they worship in my particular flavor of Christianity or not. I believe this is why the Lord is moving for unity among Christians, not among Christian denominations. We are designed for diversity and intended to remain different. Our choices for mode of worship and our belief in non-essential doctrines cannot be, and must not be, a means for the enemy to introduce division. Everyone who has received Jesus Christ as Lord, by faith through grace, is *in Christ*.

And we *must* accept them as our brothers and sisters in Christ if we are ever to walk in a unity that will express HIS GLORY.

Chapter 8

✜

FOR THE SAKE OF THE GLORY

We all have them. A person who is so close to our heart that we would do anything for them. Anything!

I started to write an example here. But as I did, I realized that I felt very uncomfortable sharing any of the things I have done which might be good examples. They were personal and private things, and every one I began to write about sounded too braggadocios. My wife recently shared an observation on an author she is reading by saying, "He bothers me. Every bad example he gives is about someone else, while every good example is about himself."

Perhaps that's our problem in a nutshell. We all see the best in ourselves, and far too frequently have such a difficult time seeing it in others. We tend to see our motives as pure, our intentions as good, our desires as minimal, our needs as most necessary, our insights as brilliant, our efforts as selfless, and the list could go on and on. Allowing that perspective brings us to this conclusion regarding our faith: If the way I choose to worship Jesus Christ is *the right way*, then the way you choose to worship Him *must* be the wrong way (or, at the very least, not the best way).

It seems rather harsh when you read it on the page of a book, doesn't it? But there it is. We put ourselves in the position of receiving the glory all too quickly. We're glory thieves! We act as though we deserve the glory for all of our wonderful choices, and most especially, for our choice of the proper way to worship Jesus in the midst of the so many others who have gotten it all wrong.

We believe there are others, of course, who've made the right choice about how to worship and serve Jesus, too. Most of the time we see them as the wise and sanctified persons who have joined our denomination, movement, communion, fellowship, association, or whatever title we've given it. (Well, to be totally frank, not *all* of them. We have our doubts about certain persons, even certain leaders, in our camp.) But the core of *our group* are the glorious ones.

It sounds so absurd when you write it down. Even as I wrote it, I could almost hear the voices being raised to object, "THAT'S not what I think at all, bishop. You've got it totally wrong!" Unfortunately, I can't judge what a person thinks. That's completely the realm of God. So I'm left judging how a person acts. And, by the way, so is the world—looking on and wondering if we Christians have *anything* in our lives that would make them want to change anything in theirs. And when the world looks at how the Church acts, they see us fighting one another and proclaiming our own glory. They see us refusing to welcome one another for some of the most absurd and selfish of reasons. They can see that we don't really love one another. So why on Earth would they believe us when we claim to bring them a message of transforming love and faith?

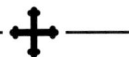

> When the world looks at how the Church acts, they see us fighting one another and proclaiming our own glory.

It's quite a sad condemnation, really, when Paul is so clear to teach us that "the only thing that counts is faith expressing itself through love."[118] Think about it, the ONLY THING that matters! Paul went even further in pressing the critical importance of us acting in love when he gave a pretty impressive list of things that mean absolutely nothing without love. I don't know how many readers of this book would be on a list of those who have moved mountains by their faith, have the ability to fathom all mysteries and knowledge, or have given all they possess to the poor. I do presume the list would be rather short, however. (For sure, I know that I wouldn't be on it!) But Paul makes it clear that, even if you made it onto THAT list, unless the actions are a faith-filled expression of Christ's love, it amounts

---
[118] Galatians 5:6

to nothing,[119] because "the *only* thing that counts is faith expressing itself through love" (emphasis added).

When the Gospels bring us to the table in the upper room and let us share the Last Supper with the apostles, they give us a glimpse of an aspect of Christ expressing His faith in love, and they do so in a manner that is hardly spoken about in the earlier accounts of His ministry. Matthew, Mark, Luke, and John all give us pages of examples of His selfless love for others. They share a multitude of His miracles and relate dozens of His interactions with everyone from teachers of the law, to demoniacs and tax collectors. But they seldom give us the content of Jesus' prayers.

They tell us *that* He prayed, of course. In the pages of the Gospels we learn of all-night prayer sessions. We find that Jesus often withdrew to lonely places and prayed.[120] We are told that very early in the morning, while it was still dark, Jesus would get up, find a quiet place, and pray.[121]

He didn't just pray alone, of course. He also taught the disciples how to pray when they asked. Luke tells us, "One day Jesus was praying in a certain place. When he finished, one of his disciples said to him, 'Lord, teach us to pray, just as John taught his disciples.'"[122] Later Luke tells us that Jesus took Peter, John, and James with Him and went up onto a mountain to pray together.[123] Matthew shows us how Jesus prayed for children.[124]

But we aren't often told *what* He prayed.

Once in a while, we get a glimpse into what Jesus prays, but it's quite rare. What Jesus says to the Father, as He stands in front of Lazarus' tomb, is more of a comment than a prayer. The same could be said of His prayer in Matthew 11:25-26. It's only in Gethsemane and in the upper room that we are given any indication of what Jesus prays. And that, in and of itself, makes these words of our Lord all the more significant.

Our most intimate exposure to the prayer life of Jesus, the Messiah, comes from the Last Supper. For twenty-six magnificent verses in John 17, Jesus pours out His heart to His Father, and we get to listen in. And, as we do, one theme is presented over and over again, as though Jesus is turning

---

[119] 1 Corinthians 13:1-3
[120] Luke 5:16
[121] Mark 1:35
[122] Luke 11:1
[123] Luke 9:28
[124] Matthew 19:13

a diamond in the flickering lamp light to show the different colors of its refractions. It is the concept of GLORY.

From the time I introduced the word *communion* in chapter one, I have been building upon that concept throughout this book. But if there is another word that should ring solidly in the hearts of every believer, it is the word GLORY. Moreover, the two are inextricably intertwined. In John 17, we see Jesus Himself ties the three concepts of our unity, the display of the glory of God, and the salvation of the world together in His prayer.

Let's read Christ's words, as He pours out His heart to the Father in John 17:

> After Jesus said this, He looked toward heaven and prayed: "Father, the time has come. Glorify Your Son, that Your Son may glorify You. For You granted Him authority over all people that He might give eternal life to all those You have given Him. Now this is eternal life: that they may know You, the only true God, and Jesus Christ, whom You have sent. I have brought You glory on earth by completing the work You gave Me to do. And now, Father, glorify Me in Your presence with the glory I had with You before the world began.
>
> "I have revealed You to those whom You gave me out of the world. They were Yours; You gave them to Me and they have obeyed your word. Now they know that everything You have given Me comes from You. For I gave them the words You gave Me and they accepted them. They knew with certainty that I came from You, and they believed that You sent Me.
>
> "I pray for them. I am not praying for the world, but for those You have given Me, for they are Yours. All I have is Yours, and all You have is Mine. And glory has come to Me through them. I will remain in the world no longer, but they are still in the world, and I am coming to You. Holy Father, protect them by the power of Your name—the name You gave Me—so that they may be one as We are one. While I was with them, I protected them and kept them safe by that name You gave me.

None has been lost except the one doomed to destruction so that Scripture would be fulfilled.

"I am coming to You now, but I say these things while I am still in the world, so that they may have the full measure of My joy within them. I have given them Your word and the world has hated them, for they are not of the world any more than I am of the world. My prayer is not that You take them out of the world but that You protect them from the evil one. They are not of the world, even as I am not of it. Sanctify them by the truth; Your word is truth. As You sent me into the world, I have sent them into the world. For them I sanctify myself, that they too may be truly sanctified.

"My prayer is not for them alone. I pray also for those who will believe in Me through their message, that all of them may be one, Father, just as You are in Me and I am in You. May they also be in Us so that the world may believe that You have sent Me. I have given them the glory that You gave Me, that they may be one as We are one: I in them and You in Me. May they be brought to complete unity to let the world know that You sent Me and have loved them even as You have loved Me.

"Father, I want those You have given Me to be with Me where I am, and to see My glory, the glory You have given Me because You loved Me before the creation of the world.

"Righteous Father, though the world does not know You, I know You, and they know that You have sent Me. I have made You known to them, and will continue to make You known in order that the love You have for Me may be in them and that I Myself may be in them."

Stop! Some of you just "skimmed" through the words of Christ's prayer. Perhaps because you believe that you are already familiar with John 17. (In fact, a few of you likely skipped the reading of John 17 entirely!) Don't rob yourself here.

In fact, let me suggest something that I hope will unlock the impact of this passage for you. You'll need to find a quiet place where you can be undisturbed for this little experiment. Take your Bible and open it to John 17. Here is what I want you to do:

STAND UP and begin to read the chapter aloud. But don't read it as if you were called upon to read it in a Bible study or a church service. I want you to imagine that you are auditioning for the lead role in a movie on the life of Christ, and the director has asked you to give John 17 as a dramatic reading.

In other words, read it as if *you* were Jesus. Read it aloud with the same passion, the same heart as if you were Jesus pouring His heart out to the Father, knowing that you'd be leaving for the Garden of Gethsemane as soon as you finish praying.

Okay, do it now.

You see, when you read it like *that*, something comes to the fore. You are struck with the intensity—focused upon the element of Christ's glory! *No one deserves glory more than Jesus.* For the sake of the glory, Jesus left heaven for Earth. He did not consider His equality with God something to be held onto and grasped, but instead, He emptied Himself and took the form of a servant.[125] He came and humbled Himself, even willingly accepting the shameful death of a criminal.

For the sake of the glory, He was reviled without mercy and executed without justice. His body was hung naked at a crossroads for the passerby to revile and then quickly dumped into a borrowed grave. So quickly, in fact, they didn't even have sufficient time to properly prepare His body for burial. Even after His death, the lies about Him continued. The accusations the Jewish leaders made against His followers caused the Roman governor to approve the posting of a *custodia* of guards, to make sure the grave remained sealed.

The Father looked on and witnessed the loving obedience of the Son. He, above all, knew the price being paid. It was a price so costly that we'll never fully understand the depth of the cost on this side of heaven. It was the price that purchased our salvation, true. But it was also the price that secured the declaration of Jesus' eternal glory.

---

[125] Philippians 2:6-11

Our Lord's willingness to sacrifice His life was the reason that "God highly exalted Him, and bestowed on Him the name which is above every name." Because He laid down His life, "at the name of Jesus every knee will bow, of those who are in heaven and on earth and under the earth, and every tongue will confess that Jesus Christ is Lord, to the glory of God the Father."[126]

Christ's prayer in John 17 totally revolves around the manifestation of His glory. At the Cana wedding, Jesus told His mother that His time had not yet come. When His brothers encouraged Jesus to go up to Jerusalem for the Feast of Tabernacles, He told them the right time for Him had not come yet. Jesus escaped physical attacks in Nazareth and the temple courts because it was not His time. But on this night, Jesus said, "the hour has come." Jesus prayed to the Father, "Glorify Me together with Yourself, with the glory which I had with You before the world was."[127]

And, oh, the glory Jesus had before the world began! Jesus was glorified with the Father in heaven before He ever came to the earth. The glory Jesus possessed was a critical element of His ministry here on Earth. Make no mistake: That same glory is a critical element of our ministry as well, if our ministry is to be effective. The Father gave Jesus glory in heaven, and because of the glory He received in heaven, He also had authority on Earth. Glory was the means through which the Father delivered authority to the Son.

That authority was the key to Jesus being able to offer eternal life to those who would believe in Him. In verse two, Jesus says the Father "granted Him authority over all people that He might give eternal life." Did you catch the connection there? The glory is the *means* of the authority. And the authority opens the door for eternal life. Jesus continued by saying, "Now this is eternal life: that they may know You, the only true God, and Jesus Christ, whom You have sent." The glory Jesus had, the glory expressed in His ministry, the glory seen in His miracles, His wisdom, His character—these are the elements of glory that allowed the Messiah to offer eternal life to you and me.

Christ's glory draws us into eternal life, where we come into an

---
[126] Philippians 2:9-11 (NASB)
[127] John 17:5 (NKJV)

intimate relationship with the Father. From God's perspective, salvation is all about a restored relationship. By offering eternal life to the world, whom the Father loves, Jesus was returning glory to the Father. His obedience to fulfill the mission His Father had given Him, gave Jesus something to offer the Father, something to glorify His holy name.

Jesus claimed that He brought glory to the Father on Earth by completing the work the Father had given Him to do. It all began with the Father speaking the Word to the Son. Then the Word became flesh and dwelt among us.[128] Jesus gave His disciples the words that were given to Him by the Father. The disciples accepted them. That's why they knew with certainty that Jesus had come from the Father, why they were able to believe that He had been sent from above.

This same aspect must be seen in our ministry to the world! If, as they hear our words, the world does not see the manifestations of God's glory, how are they going to be put in a position to believe? The glory must open their eyes. Once they believe and accept the words of Christ, they, too, will become part of the family of God. They, too, will know the Father and Jesus Christ Whom He sent. They, too, will know eternal life. Their relationships with the Father and the Son will be restored.

Because they accepted the word, the disciples could perceive His glory. Not all of it, to be sure. That is why Jesus prayed in verse 24, "Father, I want those You have given Me to be with Me where I am, and to see My glory, the glory You have given Me because you loved Me before the foundation of the world." He wanted the disciples to be able to see the fullness of His glory. It was in perceiving and beginning to comprehend His glory that the disciples came to know Jesus was the Messiah they waited for. That's what Jesus *Christ* means! Jesus is His given name. Christ, the Greek for the Anointed One, is His title. The Anointed One is the Messiah! This was a proclamation by Jesus. Because they had received the words He had given them, the apostles knew for sure Jesus was the Messiah. The world did not know, but they did.

And because they knew what the world did not, it was critical they remain in the world. They had to deliver the message of eternal life. The message of the Father was glorifying Jesus and offering forgiveness of sins

---

[128] John 1:14

in Him and His name. It was a message designed to open their eyes, so that they might see through eyes of faith; see the truth of the message that would deliver unto them the knowledge of eternal life.

And so Jesus prayed. He prayed not that the Father would take His disciples out of the world, but that they would be protected from the evil one. He prayed that they would be sanctified by the truth of His Word. Because His Word is truth, they could go into the world with His truth and change it. That's why Jesus sent them into the world. That's why Jesus chose to sanctify Himself, so they, too, could be truly sanctified! They were sent by Jesus in the same way the Father had sent Jesus. Their mission was the same as His, to walk in total unity in order to display the glory of the Father. And our mission is no different!

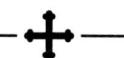

> Our mission is to walk in total unity in order to display the glory of the Father.

Jesus was in unity with His Father, He, therefore, displayed the glory of the Father to the world. This is why Jesus prayed that we would be one with Him, just as the Father was one with Him! He said, "Father may they all be one, just as You are in Me and I am in You. May they also be in Us *so that the world may believe You have sent Me. I have given them the glory that You gave Me, that they may be one as We are one*" (emphasis added). Until we obey the commandment Jesus gave us, until we deliberately choose to walk in the unity of the blood of Christ, we will never be in a position to display the glory Christ so focused on, which He prayed for in John 17.

We have focused on unity for unity's sake for far too long. It's not about unity alone. It's about unity with the Father, unity with the Son, unity with the Holy Spirit—so that Christ's prayer for unity will empower us to display His glory! It is only through the display of loving glory that people are confronted with a message which brings eternal life! This is why the Father sent the Son into the world. The Father loves the world, even as He loves the Son. Christ has given us His Word so that we might have the full measure of joy He had in obeying the Father.

Obedience, glory, and authority are all tied together. They are like a three-fold cord. The Father gave the Son glory, and then sent Him out with authority. The Son has given us glory, and He then sends us out with authority. Jesus said, "All authority on heaven and earth are given to Me, go therefore and make disciples!"[129] We are designed to display the glory of God in a dark and sin-ruled world.

And once we have obeyed and our time of service is complete, He brings us up to heaven, so that we may see His glory—the glory added unto Him through our obedience, the glory added unto Him by the Father working through us. This is the very glory added unto Him because we chose to be united, to be one, to be perfected in unity as He prayed in verse 23: "So that the world may know!" The world *must* know that the Father sent the Son. The world *must* know that eternal life is found only in Christ, and "there is no other name under heaven given to men by which we must be saved."[130] And He sanctified us in that name, giving us power and authority in our unity, so that He could send us into the world.

Look at the interlocking dependencies of verse twenty-one. The Father is in the Son. And so, the Son is also in the Father. Because of this, the disciples are in both the Father and the Son. Our being in the Father and the Son is designed to bring us to a place of unity. In that place, we are able to reflect the glory needed to show forth the eternal gospel. The world sees the love and the unity in the Body, and so the world believes that the Father has sent the Son.

Without us walking in love—in determined and deliberate unity, without us being sanctified by the truth—the world will not believe. But note this well: When the world does not believe, it's not because of the Father, nor is it because of the Son. Neither the Father nor the Son has failed. It's because of *us* the world does not believe!

It is we who refuse to obey Christ's command to love one another, as He has loved us. We are the ones who choose to find almost every convenient excuse as grounds for division. Somehow, we have come to the conclusion that we don't really need to love one another in order to be called Christians. We can choose our ways instead of His.

When we made that choice, the glory departed. It's only as we manifest the *love* of Christ that we have access to the *glory* of Christ. It's only as we

---

[129] Matthew 28:18
[130] Acts 4:12

stand in unity that we have the authority to proclaim the gospel with power. And only when the gospel is proclaimed with power does Christ move in such a way that even more glory is added to His already glorious name!

When we operate in unity the dead are raised! When we operate in unity the sick are healed! When we operate in unity those who have been wounded are finally able to forgive! Our unity is built on the basis of love—Christ's love!

Love is the key. God so loved the world that He sent His Son. The Son loved the world so much, He equipped and sent *us*. He proclaimed that His obedience had given Him all authority in heaven and on Earth. Then He gave it to us and sent us in His name.

It's our deliberate unity and love for the body (through our obedience) that gives us the authority to proclaim the message of the gospel in power. Only our fruitfulness will follow us into heaven, placing gifts in our hands that will allow us to add glory to the already glorious name of Jesus Christ.

The Father gave the Son His glory. The Son gave the disciples His glory. He did it so that we may be one. Jesus was perfecting unity in the disciples so the world would know that the Father loves the world. So the world would know the Father sent His Son.

The world doesn't know the Father; Jesus knows the Father. So Jesus revealed the Father to His disciples. And the disciples then knew the Father had sent Jesus. Jesus made the Father's name known to them. This is the key to the eternal life He offers. Only as the love of the Father was seen in the Son, only as the love of the Father and the Son was seen in the disciples, would the name of Christ be lifted up in this world.

When we lift up the name of Jesus, when we choose love, when we choose unity, then we can bring glory to Christ. And it's all about the glory! That is the bottom line.

The most important outcome for the gospel is that Jesus be glorified in heaven before the Father with the glory He had before the world began. He's worthy of our obedience. He is worthy of our dedicated service. But most of all, He is worthy of the glory.

It's *all* for the sake of the glory!

Chapter 9

---✢---

DEALING WITH THE DIFFERENCES

Kadin is a young Muslim man in his twenties, I've come to know him during my travels in Israel. Kadin's father is a Muslim, but his mother is Jewish. Sadly, though perhaps not surprisingly, his parents decided to get a divorce while Kadin was quite young. When they did, Kadin and his twin brother, Mohammed, were separated. Kadin remained with his father and was raised a Muslim. His twin brother was renamed Gilad and was raised a Jew by his mother.

Some time ago, Kadin decided to go on a three day weekend trip to Eilat, the popular vacation spot at the southern tip of Israel. Since Kadin's brother, Gil, was employed in Eilat, they took advantage of the opportunity to spend time together. On Kadin's final morning in Eilat, he brought up an issue of failed familial hospitality which had begun to bother him. (You see, in the culture of the Middle East, visiting family is *always* invited to your home.)

"Gil, you and I have been here three days, but you've not invited me to your house?"

Gil's reply was both stunning and swift.

"Of course not," he sneered. "You're an *Arab*!"

I remember sitting there in a state of shocked surprise when Kadin, with tears in his eyes, recounted this painful incident. Of course Kadin was deeply hurt by his brother's rejection, and naturally, he became quite angry. But my shock was focused on a totally different element.

This was his *twin brother* speaking! They were biologically and genetically identical, yet Gil had set up an arbitrary line of separation, based solely upon external choices and circumstances. Worse yet, Gil was utterly unable to see past the artificial barriers established by the choices his parents and his culture had made, even though they were completely baseless and illogical. In many ways we have done exactly the same thing in the Church.

Bethlehem College & Seminary's Chancellor, John Piper, said: "God's family, which comes into being by regeneration, is more central and more lasting than the human family that comes into being by procreation." We are God's family, "blood brothers" washed in the precious blood of the Lord Jesus Christ. While we are, in fact, more intimately and indissolubly related than a natural family ever could be, we have allowed choices made by our parents in the faith (our leaders) and our faith culture (our denominations) to erect false barriers.

I am well aware that many, if not most, will argue that these barriers are neither baseless nor illogical. While discussing these barriers to unity with a friend just last week, he asked me "How can I have unity with someone who does not see the Scripture as the inerrant Word of God? If they don't accept God's Word, how can I accept them?" To him, this seems like a barrier which cannot be overcome. To me, it appears quite differently. Let me share an illustration to explain why.

When a baby is born it utterly lacks the skills, knowledge, and education it will ultimately need to survive and thrive. It is completely dependent upon its family to care for it while it learns and grows. It is in the context of family that the child receives everything he needs for life, and in so receiving, hopefully grows, over time, to a fruitful and productive maturity.

It would be absurd to push the child outside of the family and insist he only be recognized and accepted as part of the family when he has developed full maturity on his own. It would be just as foolish to insist that the child was only *really* part of the family if he met some particular external criteria, such as joining the same political party as his parents, or living in the same town as they did for the rest of his life.

The process of growing in truth and knowledge requires relationship.

It requires communication. It requires time. And, as any parent can tell you, there are times when a child can even be the teacher to the parent, for no set of parents is the perfect embodiment of all truth. There are also times the behavior of the child will need the correction of a parent, because none of our children are perfect either.

So when another believer in Christ does not hold to our specific set of beliefs on a key doctrine, such as the inspiration of Scripture, or how they see the real presence of Christ in the Eucharist, or the proper mode of baptism, or the present-day operation of the gifts of the Holy Spirit, or any of dozens of other doctrines, the answer is not to cut off all communication with them and curse their ignorance. Isn't the better approach to recognize, first of all, that *in Christ we are only one Body*, we are tied together on the basis of Christ's blood. To build upon that, both communion and communication will be required to resolve these differences.

If you choose to ignore the basis of His blood, upon which all believers are brought into the same family, and allow it to eliminate either your communion or your communication with the Body; then you make your practices, or your conditions, the foundation of your faith in Christ. This is in opposition to the standard He Himself has set. If, on the other hand, you insist on beginning with the basis of the blood of Christ, which has purchased us, cleansed us from sin, and made us a part of the Church and, therefore, includes us in the family of God—the discussion takes an entirely different tack.

Note please: I am speaking of differences that relate to how to apply the Scriptures in our lives in the practice of living out our faith. This logic does not apply to those who insist on continuing to walk in a lifestyle of sin that is diametrically opposed to the Scriptures themselves. For example, adultery is clearly identified as a sin in the Scriptures. So if a person insists on calling themselves a Christian while maintaining a life filled with adulterous relationships, there is no way to walk "in unity" with that person. The role of the Church has always been to love the sinner, hate the sin, and be a voice for freedom from sin.

The ministry of the Church is a ministry of reconciliation, leading people trapped in the bondage of sin to freedom. James makes it clear that sin is a trap from the enemy, a snare set to capture and then destroy us. He warns us that "after desire has conceived, it gives birth to sin; and sin, when it is full-grown, gives birth to death."[131] True love is never willing to leave the one who is loved ensnared. This, then, is why the Church's call is to lovingly welcome the sinner and share the message of freedom, which is found in Christ. In living out this ministry of reconciliation, we are sharing the life-giving message that God is reconciling the world to Himself and not counting our sins against us. That is true freedom!

Accept the sinner without affirming the sin. Jesus did this over and over again throughout His ministry. Jesus lovingly called people to find freedom in Him, abandoning the sins that were controlling and ruining their lives. "So if the Son sets you free, you will be free indeed."[132]

In the previous example, the love of Christ is best demonstrated by lovingly showing the person trapped in adultery that, no matter how much pleasure the sin may currently bring, the sin is actually destroying his life, destroying his lover's life and destroying their families. He needs to see that the love of Christ offers to set them free from this sin. The Church's role is to walk each of the sinners into a place of forgiveness, healing, and wholeness in Christ; which will bring true life, true freedom, and true love. Not the counterfeit love they are currently walking in, which will actually lead to destruction. Not the empty pleasure that the enemy offers to replace true joy.

I have seen the love of Christ set people free from addiction to drugs, alcoholism, pornography, homosexuality and other sexual perversions, as well bitter hatred. NOTHING is too great for the love of Christ to conquer. The Church must love the sinner enough to walk with him as the Lord frees him from sin. Jesus was known to associate with tax collectors, prostitutes, and other sinners. But He called them *out* of the sinful life which ensnared them. He led them to the freedom of holiness.

The process by which the Church is to deal with sin is clearly laid out in several places in the Scriptures, and this book is not a treatise on how to do so. But one thing is sadly clear, when one who calls himself a brother deliberately decides to continue in his sin, in spite of the clear

---

[131] James 1:15
[132] John 8:36

teaching of the Word of God and the admonition of the Church, he is *not* to be accepted within the community of faith.[133] But even here the goal is love. The goal of expelling the sinful brother is to force him to confront his sin. As Paul makes clear, when the sinful brother has dealt with his sin, he is to be received with the same open arms of love that were forced to push him away.[134] In this manner, the pure power of love is brought to bear upon the sin and the sinner. I give a deeper analysis of this process in the epilog.

To continue the illustration of the baby, the ministry of the Church is like that of the parent who must have the maturity to raise the newborn child in love, while changing his messy diapers, day after day. The parent understands that the goal is to eliminate the need for the diaper, and the child must learn this as well. The key is the patient and consistent input from the parent.

John put it this way, "If we walk in the Light as He Himself is in the Light, we have fellowship with one another, and the blood of Jesus His Son cleanses us from all sin."[135] This is the Church dealing with sin and applying the Word of God to transform the lives of believers. This is the Church allowing the blood of Christ to cleanse us. It is the blood of Christ that flows through His Body, cleansing the filth and removing that which would kill us if it were to remain. When we choose to ignore the basis of blood which joins us all in Him, when we allow sin to cloud our vision and foul our lives, we become far too willing to believe the lies the enemy puts before us to increase our divisions.

Not too long ago, I was speaking with the leader of a large messianic congregation in Israel who warned me to stay away from the leader of another major Christian group. The basis for his warning was a heretical statement the other leader had supposedly made. The first brother was convinced that the other leader was deliberately attempting to mislead a large element of the Body of Christ, or at the very least, was being deceived by satan for that same purpose.

The only problem was that my Israeli friend was relying upon a published report, taking at face value what the media *said* the other leader had said. (He had read it on the Internet, so it must be true, right?) I had

---
[133] 1 Corinthians 5:9-11
[134] 2 Corinthians 2:7
[135] 1 John 1:7 (NASB)

read the same report, researched it, and found out that—shock of shocks—the media had totally misrepresented what this leader had actually said. When I challenged my friend on his false assumption and presented the evidence of my research, he was unwilling to re-examine the evidence. The problem was clear to me. This misreported incident matched his historical misperception of this church leader, and so he was naturally predisposed to accept the false claim of the Internet story. It was simply easier and more comfortable to believe the lie.

So how can we deal with the differences, both real and imaginary, that have been so effectively dividing us? Is there a possible path forward towards a greater unity? I believe there is.

First of all, let's be clear and remind ourselves about the basis upon which claim our inherent unity. It is salvation by grace, through faith alone in the finished work of Christ on the cross. Once a person has received Christ, they are part of the same Body as us. Like it or not. But as Bishop J. C. Ryle, the first bishop of Liverpool England, so wisely noted, "Unity without the gospel is a worthless unity; it is the very unity of hell." We claim Christ and His work of grace in our lives as the basis and foundation for our unity—nothing more, nothing less.

And just to be completely clear, our determination for unity in the Body of Christ, under the gospel, should never be confused with our efforts to build and maintain channels of communication with unbelievers in order to share the gospel. There are those who confuse interfaith dialog with a diabolical attempt to establish one world religion. In fact, this is a common knee-jerk response whenever the topic of Christian unity is seriously discussed. But evangelism and ecumenism are vastly different things. The unity of the Body of Christ can only exist *in* the Body of Christ.

Of course, there are many matters upon which the Christian Church can and should cooperate with unbelievers. When a natural disaster strikes, for example, it makes no difference whether the person standing next to you handing out soup and blankets is a Methodist or a Muslim. Combatting child sexual exploitation can be effectively done by Baptists or Buddhists. These are avenues for mutual cooperation and serve as means for opening dialog and sharing the gospel while doing good. They provide the bridges for evangelism, but they are definitely not a statement of unity *in Christ*.

(For the record, I want to publically admit here that I *am* totally in favor of one world religion—the one intended by Jesus Christ. He commanded His followers to "Go and make disciples of all nations, baptizing them in the name of the Father and of the Son and of the Holy Spirit, and teaching them to obey everything I have commanded you."[136])

Next, having begun "in Christ," we must accept the realization that we are supposed to be different. The teaching of Scripture is abundantly clear. Because we are a Body, we have different functions. Eyes, ears, hands, feet, tongues and elbows are all different, yet all necessary. Some parts are given more honor, some parts less; but none are unnecessary. These differences will be seen both in things one group will choose to accept, as well as in things another group may choose not to accept, or will choose to see differently. Some of us in Christ love to eat meat, others of us in Christ choose not to do so. Paul makes it clear that the ones who do eat meat are not to look down upon the ones who do not, and vice versa.[137] The Greek word for "holiness" is not *vegan*.

> We must accept the realization that we are supposed to be different.

Some Christians will be open to the practice of speaking in tongues, while other believers will not. The Scriptures have words of wisdom for both groups. The former are encouraged to understand that not all will speak in tongues,[138] while the latter are warned not to forbid the practice.[139] We are different! More to the point, we are different *by design*. God intends us to be different, and He wants it that way. This should encourage us and allow us to rejoice in His divine design for diversity. I don't want everybody in the Church to be cookie-cutter Christians who all dress, talk, and pray exactly the same. Apparently neither does the Lord.

Since we know that we are designed to be different, we can understand that *our differences do not need to divide us*. One of my sons is introverted and analytical, another is extroverted and creative. These differences do

---
[136] Matthew 28:19-20
[137] Romans 14:1-10
[138] 1 Corinthians 12:30
[139] 1 Corinthians 14:39

not divide them, and they certainly don't question whether they need to break up our family into two different families! We remain one family, while recognizing and celebrating the differences among us. It is embracing and enjoying our differences that brings zest to living life together. We're different, we recognize it, and we enjoy it. The love we share allows us maintain our relationship, in spite of our differences.

Isn't it high time that we stop allowing the effective witness of the Body of Christ to be marred by our lack of love and acceptance for one another? There is a great deal of confusion about the message of truth in the world today. I've been sharing my faith with one particular young man for several years now. He regularly comes to my church. He's participated in (and even excelled at) Bible memory challenges. But he absolutely does not accept the gospel of Jesus Christ. His argument for refusing to do so is telling. He doesn't believe the Bible is the Word of God, and when he compares its teachings to the way people who claim to be followers of Christ live, he sees nothing compelling him to change his mind. Because of a lack of living evidence to the contrary, he sees the Bible as nothing more than a collection of myths.

But what if he were to be confronted with a vibrant group of people who were characterized by a selfless and dynamic love for one another? What if he came to church and saw people powerfully moved by their faith, living lives in a unity that reflected the glory of God? What if, day after day, as he walked among those of us who claim to be born-again in Christ, he were to see prayers answered, people healed, demons cast out, and the dead raised back to life? Can you imagine what impact that would have on him?

You don't have to imagine it! You can read about it in the Gospels and the book of the Acts of the Apostles. That was what people living the Christian faith in unity looked like and lived like, and it turned the world upside down. If the Church would stop fighting one another and begin fighting the good fight of faith, we could turn our world upside down today, too.

But we don't. And that is the reason the world cannot recognize us! We don't look or act differently from anyone else the world compares us to. So, why should they believe our life-changing message of love and forgiveness?

Joni Eareckson Tada observed that, "Believers are never told to become one; we already are one and are expected to act like it." Jesus said, "By this everyone will know that you are My disciples, if you love one another."[140] We don't and so they don't. It's really that simple. When we refuse to love one another the world can't tell the people who ARE Jesus' disciples from the people who are not. We look just like the world, and we don't care. We are lukewarm and loving it.

What a shame that we continue to let our differences divide us. We separate over such weighty matters as blue or red covers for our pew Bibles, grape juice or wine for communion, clerical collar or casual wear for the preacher, and on and on and on *ad nauseum*. And while we allow our differences to divide us, the world passes to a Christ-less eternity, because our behavior makes it impossible to differentiate the church from the world. We refuse to be known by our love for one another.

> The Body must be different if it is to accomplish all that is needed.

Recognizing that He designed us to be different can change all of that. Love will change the way the world sees us. When we deliberately choose to love one another, *everyone* will know that we are His disciples. He said so.

Like a healthy family, we can operate together and overlook our non-essential differences. The Body *must be* different if it is to accomplish all that is needed. The apostle Paul makes this abundantly clear when he asks, "Are all apostles? Are all prophets? Are all teachers? Do all work miracles? Do all have gifts of healing? Do all speak in tongues? Do all interpret?"[141] Of course not!

As he said earlier in the chapter,

> If the whole body were an eye, where would the sense of hearing be? If the whole body were an ear, where would the

---

[140] John 13:35
[141] 1 Corinthians 12:29–30

sense of smell be? But in fact God has arranged the parts in the body, every one of them, just as He wanted them to be. If they were all one part, where would the body be? As it is, there are many parts, but one body. [142]

Since we are many parts but one Body, we can operate together the way a body is supposed to. Each part can do its part. We need not be concerned that the other parts are doing their part differently than the way we do our part, but we're to recognize that we need all of the parts to function as they were designed to function. I'm pleased that my body has both a heart and a pair of eyes. I need them both. Neither do I wish them to try and fulfill the role the other was designed for, since having eyes inside of my chest, trying to pump blood, would defeat the very purpose of the eyes.

The Church needs people with Spirit-inspired words of wisdom and words of knowledge. The Body needs those with gifts of healing and miracles. We need those among us who can distinguish between various types of spirits. Apostles, prophets, evangelists, pastors, and teachers, with their different ministries, are designed to equip us all for the works of service that will build up the Body of Christ. It is in *working together* that we are built up. Paul said that "this will continue until we all come to such unity in our faith and knowledge of God's Son that we will be mature in the Lord, measuring up to the full and complete standard of Christ."[143] Our unity is a sign of our maturity. You know what that makes our dis-unity, right?

When we work together and each of us fulfills our God-given role, we will impact the world in a way that we never could in our present state of division. D.L. Moody said, "I have never yet known the Spirit of God to work where the Lord's people were divided." In case you haven't noticed, the world desperately needs us to be the Church; and the world isn't being won over by our division and petty bickering. We have the real answer, the only answer to the darkness gripping the world today. We need to let them see it in us.

The Church working together in the love of Christ is the answer to

---

[142] 1 Corinthians 12:17–20
[143] Ephesians 4:13 (NLT)

poverty. The Church working together in the love of Christ is the answer to the illegal drug trade and the lives it destroys. The Church working together in the love of Christ is the answer—period. The light ALWAYS overcomes the darkness.

More than just overlooking the differences we have, we can *value* the differences in order to maximize the accomplishment of the mission. Recently, some of my sons and I built an addition onto our house to make an in-law suite for my wife's mom. Because I had some experience in framing and building, it was a project we were mostly able to accomplish by our own efforts. But the framing of the roof rafters was a particularly challenging element, and so I decided to hire someone to come over and help us get that part of the job done. I didn't need a plumber or an electrician, even though they are both in the building trades. I didn't need a pilot, or a web designer, or a physician. I needed an experienced framing carpenter, so that's what I hired.

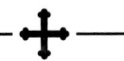

> More than just overlooking the differences we have, we can value the differences in order to maximize the accomplishment of the mission.

The carpenter I hired wasn't perfect. He had a few personality quirks which we didn't exactly enjoy. I didn't find some of his jokes particularly hilarious. I'm sure there were more than a few things about us that rubbed him the wrong way, too. But I had a mission, I needed a roof. He had a mission, he needed a paycheck. We both chose to focus on the task at hand and ignore the minor aggravating elements in order to get the job done. After a few days of work, we got the roof framed and sheathed, and he got paid. Mission accomplished—for BOTH of us.

As we go into all the world to make disciples of all nations, there will be many different jobs to be done. Let's let each person fulfill his role and use his gifts, talents, training, education and experience, to its greatest effect, throughout the Body of Christ. As the old saying goes, "If you only have a hammer, then every problem looks like a nail." Let's not force everyone to try and fit a certain mold. God has given the Church a wide and varied diversity of gifts. And we need them all. Let's focus on the task at hand and overlook the things that would distract us from accomplishing the all-important task of winning the world to Christ.

To paraphrase Charles H. Brent, "The unity of Christendom is not a luxury but a necessity. The world will continue limping its way into hell until Christ's prayer, that all may be one, is answered. We must have unity, not at all costs but at all risks." The foundation of the gospel makes the risk of love and unity worthwhile.

Is it risky to work alongside someone who's not "part of your church?" Perhaps. But Christ gifted the whole Body, so therefore we must need the whole Body. In so doing, He chose to give a diversity of gifts. He didn't give everyone all of His gifts; none of us can do it all. Each one in the Body has a gift, and none of us is without purpose.

Valuing the different gifts allows us to use the right tool for the job. If I were to visit your church, you might ask me to teach a Sunday school class. You may invite me to preach. But if you are wise, you won't ask me to lead worship. Trust me in this! I am simply not gifted in this area. We have different gifts for a reason.

The ability to see the value in the gifting and service of others also frees us from the error of believing "if the way I choose to worship or serve Jesus Christ is the right way (and we serve or worship differently), then the way you choose to worship and serve Him *must* be the wrong way." Let's be clear. The "right way" to worship, or serve, does not exist, at least on this side of death. We will all find the perfect expression of worship as we stand before the throne of grace. But, for now, we must learn to accept and value the different gifts, callings, and expressions of biblical faith we have been given.

As we come together and work with one another (valuing the differences Christ created in us so that we can maximize our mission's success), *resist* the temptation to judge according to your own standard, even (perhaps, especially) if you feel as though your faith is stronger. The admonition of Romans 14:1 can direct us here. It says, "Accept him whose faith is weak, *without passing judgment* on disputable matters" (emphasis added). Paul then goes on to list some of the most significant faith issues of his day. Do we eat meat or not? Shall the Sabbath be held as an especially holy day, or are we to see all days as holy?

As important as these issues were to the believers of Paul's day, none of them was to be allowed to create division. Paul's focus is clearly directed to the one who believes himself to be superior, the one who is certain that his way is the correct one. "You, then, why do you judge your brother? Or why do you look down on your brother? Who are you to judge someone else's servant?"[144] I find it particularly interesting that Paul doesn't give the answer that either side would like. He doesn't say, "Of course everyone should eat meat!" He basically says, "One eats, one doesn't, so what? Don't let THAT divide you!"

Finally, when necessary, *we can choose obedience over understanding*. Christ's choices must overrule ours. In disputable matters, we are instructed to stop passing judgement upon one another.[145] But there are matters that are indisputable and for these, we must be willing even to expel one who claims to be a brother or sister but is sexually immoral, greedy, an idolater or slanderer, a drunkard or swindler.[146]

Initially, this does not seem like either love or unity, but it is! The separation done *in love* has as its goal the repentance and eventual restoration of the offender. It is the love in which the punishment is delivered that will keep the door open. Unity requires that we be as ready to expel as we are to receive, and it further requires that we be *especially* ready to forgive and to receive back once again.[147]

Our obedience demonstrates His Lordship. Our obedience, performed in love, adds a character to our unity which reflects His glory. Our unity is Christ-centered and gospel-based. Jesus calls us to be characterized by love—but not an abstract, worldly love. Our lives, our relationships, and our communion with one another are to be characterized by the type of love He expressed for the Father. Holy, determined to obey, intent on accomplishing all to which He was called.

This is the type of love envisioned even by some of the severest judgments of the Old Testament, as my friend Rabbi Chaim Cunin shared

---

[144] Romans 14:10, 5 (Paraphrase mine)
[145] Romans 14:3
[146] 1 Corinthians 5:11
[147] 2 Corinthians 2:6-11

with me not too long ago. He wrote a commentary offering rabbinical insights into the Torah portion assigned to be read that day. He shared an interesting insight into Leviticus 13, which requires that it be a *priest* who examines a person with a rash or a sore or a moldy article of clothing to determine if he must be expelled from among the people. Rabbi Cunin says the reason it must be a priest and not just a neighbor, one of the elders, or even a Levite, is because the priests "are the spiritual heirs of the very first priest, Aaron, who was famous for promoting brotherly love among the Jewish people."

> Because of their love for their fellow Jews, the priests—while taking care not to bend the law of the Torah in any way—will make absolutely sure that the law indeed requires them to pronounce the sufferer defiled before doing so. And if the priests do have to declare a person defiled, they will do whatever it takes to declare him undefiled at the earliest possible opportunity.[148]

Even when the Word of God required them to separate a member of their community from the rest so that the spread of a defiling element could be thwarted, the priest represented and acted in the love of God. And the same priest would do all in his power to restore the person to the community of faith as soon as possible. Separation is always to be made with a deliberate eye toward restoration.

Today the Church needs to choose obedience to the clear standards of God's Word, even when that obedience requires us to place someone, in love, outside of the camp for a time. Though initially this seems opposed to the very unity and love we profess, it is actually central to it. The standard of love and unity must be protected to be preserved.

There's a word for something that is part of the body, but is actually eating away at it and destroying it. That word is CANCER. As a cancer survivor, I can tell you with certainty that cancer leaves you only two choices—eliminate the cancer or die! When the former is impossible, the latter is inevitable. Like cancer, sin offers us only those same two options.

---

[148] http://www.chabad.org/dailystudy/dailywisdom.asp?tdate=4/9/2016

I discuss the question, "How exactly does one expel someone from a close community *in love*?" in greater detail in the epilog to the book, "Dealing with Discipline," so I won't belabor the point now.

Non-denominational churches often open their communion services by saying something like this: "If you are a believer in Jesus Christ, you are welcome at this table. It is *His Table*, not ours. We are called to do this in remembrance of Him." This is intended to be an open invitation to all who call Christ their Lord, but it is also a reminder that it is He who calls us, not we who invite ourselves. And when we come at His invitation, we accept the requirements of His call.

Remember the quote from the Archbishop of Split at the beginning of chapter four? He said, "In essentials unity, in non-essentials liberty, in all things charity." How do we in the Church go about focusing upon the essentials?

The first essential is Christ's sole command to us: "A new command I give you: Love one another. As I have loved you, so you must love one another. By this everyone will know that you are My disciples, if you love one another."[149] Our signal virtue. The one thing Christ tells us will compel the world to acknowledge we are *truly* His disciples is perhaps the thing we fail at most miserably.

Andy Stanley is a well-known pastor in the greater Atlanta, Georgia area. In a series of messages entitled "Christian," he makes the argument that anyone can define the term *Christian* by any set of behaviors or choices he wishes, because the word—which is only used three times in the Bible—is never defined.[150] "You can hide behind the term 'Christianity' all day long," he tells us, "You can define it, re-define it, mis-define it and un-define it." Based upon the writings of Tacitus, he says that the term was used by outsiders to describe the "Jesus Community," and it was probably a derogatory name. Stanley asserts it was actually never used by people in the "Jesus Community" to describe themselves.

He says the term that the early believers in Jesus used most to describe themselves—in fact the term Jesus used Himself—was *disciple*. He says that a disciple is someone who is determined to be a learner, a

---

[149] John 13:34-35
[150] https://www.youtube.com/watch?v=BK6Ohz5DH0o

pupil, and adherent, an apprentice, and a follower. A disciple is one whose life's decisions are ruled by the One he is following.

Whether you agree with Andy's assessment and vocabulary or not, one point is pretty clear: Jesus called us to be His disciples. As His disciples, Jesus commanded us to love one another. Jesus clarified this command by saying that we do it in the same way He loved us. In so doing, Jesus made His expectation unequivocally clear for those who choose to follow Him. There is simply no way to misinterpret His instruction.

This difference between those who only call themselves Christians versus those who are true followers of Jesus can reach a point that would almost make you laugh, if it didn't make you want to cry even more. Take for example the story of Anne Rice, an author with over one hundred million book sales to her credit. Anne is probably best known for her series, *The Vampire Chronicles*, which included the book, *Interview With A Vampire*. In 2005, she surprised her readers by publically stating that she had abandoned years of atheism and returned to her faith in Jesus. In 2008, she shared the details of her spiritual journey in her autobiographical work, *Called Out Of Darkness*.

Then in 2010, she quit Christianity.

That's right. She just quit! Mind you, she didn't leave Jesus; she just abandoned Christianity. Here's how she put it on her Facebook page:

> For those who care, and I understand if you don't: Today I quit being a Christian. I'm out. I remain committed to Christ as always; but not to being "Christian" or to being part of Christianity. It's simply impossible for me to "belong" to this quarrelsome, hostile, disputatious, and deservedly infamous group. In the name of Christ, I quit Christianity and being Christian. Amen.[151]

When we think of terms that would best describe the group of people who were directly told by Jesus "as I have loved you, so you *must* love one another," words like quarrelsome, hostile, and disputatious shouldn't top the list. Anne put the final nail in the coffin when she explained her decision to

---

[151] Anne Rice's Facebook page, 28 July 2010 post.

Sarah Pulliam Bailey for a *Christianity Today* article. She said, "Christians have lost credibility in America as people who know how to love."

Not just in America, Anne, but all over the world.

I'm sure you've already noticed that Christ didn't leave us with a new operational strategy, a new relational insight, or a new suggestion. He said it was a new *command*. Another word for that is an order. Having served as a US Marine, I have a keen appreciation for the difference between orders and suggestions. In my experience, orders are the sort of things that commanding officers take pretty seriously. Ignoring them is likely to deliver consequences which are quite severe.

Back in the late 1970s, while I was stationed with the First Marine Brigade, we had a commanding general who loved to run. One Saturday morning, his run took him past one of the regimental headquarters buildings under his command. As he jogged past, it occurred to the general that he did not observe the sentry who was required to be standing post. Thinking that he may be on patrol behind the building, he continued his run. When he *still* didn't observe the sentry on his next pass about forty-five minutes later, he decided to investigate.

When I arrived for work at the Intelligence Office the following Monday morning, a photocopy of a hand-written note the commanding general left for the regimental commander had already been placed upon my desk. In fact, it had been placed upon every desk in the headquarters building!

The note read:

Colonel,

Contact my office no later than 0915 Monday morning and explain to me why an unidentified man wearing nothing but red PT shorts and a Marine Corps t-shirt can enter your headquarters, walk around the inside of the building, enter your office and sit at your desk long enough to write this note without being challenged by a sentry!

Harry Hagaman
Brigadier General, Commanding

It seems that, when the regimental commander arrived for work on Monday morning, he found that the commanding general had taped the original note to the chair in his office. Obviously none too pleased, the regimental commander had sent a copy of the note to every office in his command, along with a sharply-worded reminder about what happens to sentries who abandon their posts. The consequences this particular sentry faced were both unpleasant and expensive.

If Christ's only commandment to us is that we love one another the way He loved us—deliberately, intentionally, sacrificially, and with a determination to forgive and re-engage—what sort of reaction do you think we can anticipate when He returns and finds us not following His command? Not trying and failing, mind you, but straight-up deciding to simply IGNORE His direct order!

Something tells me that His reaction is going to make General Hagaman's pale in comparison. All the sentry put at risk when he deliberately disobeyed orders was the security of the Classified Materials Control Center in the headquarters of the Third Marine Regiment, the repository for documents which had been classified "Top Secret." What the Church puts at risk when we choose to deliberately disobey our orders is the operational success of the Great Commission.

You see, Christ makes it totally clear that this is how *everyone will know* that we are His disciples. It's not by what we believe, even though He surely wants us to hold to biblical beliefs. It's not by the way we dress, though our clothes should be modest and appropriate. It's not by whether we eat meat or abstain. It's whether we choose to love one another the way He loves us.

As the Church has so aptly shown, when we refuse to love one another as Christ loves us, then all of the things we do to try and fulfill the Great Commission are only sporadically effective.

Sure we've seen amazing revivals which have broken down barriers of class and race. But a decade or two later, the Church is back to business as usual. Certainly, there have been amazing evangelists who have travelled the world and even caused many (if not most) of the Christian churches in their community to work together during the large crusades. But as Charles

Spurgeon, Billy Sunday, D.L. Moody, or Billy Graham leaves town, the unity gets on the plane with them. And the world sees it and stays away in droves.

The Church has simply got to take the command of Christ seriously if we have any hope to rebuild our damaged reputation and demonstrate what an amazing change the love of Christ can truly make in our lives. When Jesus said, "You *must* love one another," He wasn't joking. He meant every word of it. He said it was a command.

That is the bottom line. This is unity for mission's sake, not unity for unity's sake. C. S. Lewis said, "If you read history you will find that the Christians who did most for the present world were precisely those who thought most of the next. It is since Christians have largely ceased to think of the other world that they have become so ineffective in this."

The key to dealing with our differences is focusing on our Master's *command* and the essentials of the mission He has charged us with.

Chapter 10

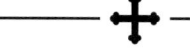

A Path Forward

096947.

That number doesn't mean anything to you. But it certainly means a lot to James "Gator" Leggett. It's the number the State of Florida assigned Leggett when they sentenced him to prison for the November 7, 1984 murder of his ex-wife, Vera.

James had a reputation for having a temper which lived up to his nickname. Gators are dangerous, unpredictable, and mean. That described James Leggett to a tee—fine one minute, then flying into a fit of rage the next.

When Vera told her family she planned to marry James, Vera's father, Jesse, was very concerned. A Methodist pastor, he remembers praying as he watched his daughter walk down the aisle, "Lord, please protect her."

Leggett's temper often got the best of him. It was not long into the marriage Vera confided to her brother, Bert, that James was beating her, even showing Bert the bruises he had left upon her back and legs. The relationship didn't last. Vera filed for divorce after three long years of abuse.

A few days after the divorce became final, James returned and once again beat his now ex-wife. Vera told Bert what had happened. Intent on protecting his sister from a repeat attack, Bert took a 12-gauge shotgun and a baseball bat with him over to his sister's home the following night. Eventually, when James did not arrive that night, Bert returned home in the early hours of the morning.

Two nights later, James arrived at Vera's house drunk, angry, and armed with a .38 caliber revolver. When Vera tried to call 911, things rapidly went from ugly to deadly. James shot his ex-wife six times before turning his now-empty revolver on himself in an attempt to take his own life.

When the police showed up on the Baker family's doorstep and informed them Vera had been murdered, Bert ran out into the driveway, dropped to his knees, and began pounding his head upon the pavement. Blaming himself for not protecting his sister, he decided, then and there, he had to take responsibility for his failure. He decided to kill James Leggett himself.

After James Leggett was sentenced to forty years in a Florida state prison, Bert made several efforts to enter the prison where Leggett was incarcerated, intending to make good on his decision to kill him. This proved fruitless. But under Florida law, James Leggett would be eligible for release in twenty years, so Bert began to plan his eventual revenge.

Bert told me, "I didn't think I was angry. I just thought I was taking care of my family. I drank a lot. I could go through a bottle of whisky in a couple of nights—a big bottle. I made Gator's release date the pin number for my ATM card. Every time I would get money out of the bank, I would remind myself, 'that's the day when he gets out, and that's when I'm going to find him and kill him.'"

But while in prison, Leggett learned that Vera's brother Bert had set out to kill him. James said, "I had made up my mind that, when I was released, I was going to kill Bert before he could kill me. So I started planning my second homicide and trying to figure out how I could kill him and get away with it."

Sixteen years into his sentence, James Leggett's temper landed him in solitary confinement for three weeks. For James, his time in "the box" was a breaking point.

"I was just so angry!" James recalled. "I was angry at life, angry at people, and angry at God. I remember that I just started yelling at God. I said, 'God, you try to talk a good game and all. You talk all this trash about how You love me. How Your Son died for me on the cross.' But I just told God, 'Where was You at when my Dad died? You've got a lot of people fooled—but not me!'"

But God wasn't finished with James. For the next seven days, God dealt with issue after issue in James' life. The Holy Spirit slowly began to remove all the barriers that years of hate and anger had built up. Leggett's heart finally broke. "I repented and accepted Christ into my life. Afterwards, I cried for seven straight days as the Holy Spirit would bring different things to my mind and then deal with them."

His final seven days in solitary, James found himself singing praises to God! "Through that time, God gave me the peace that surpasses all understanding," he said.

The James Leggett that emerged from solitary confinement was not the same James Leggett who had gone in. He *knew* that God had forgiven him, but James wondered if his ex-wife's family ever could. He decided to write Vera's parents and ask their forgiveness. "I told them how I had met Jesus, and how sorry I was for the horrible act I committed against their family, for the pain, and the loss of their beautiful daughter. I asked them to forgive me."

Vera's father said, "I'd been angry long enough. It was time to get rid of that anger. It was time to honor her memory." Vera's mother was also willing to forgive. Jesse and Fay Baker wrote to let James know that they had forgiven him.

In 2002, after serving eighteen years of his sentence, James Leggett was released from prison. A friend of the family arranged a "forgiveness visit." James came into the room, walked over to Mr. Baker and asked Jesse to forgive him for the terrible thing he had done to his family, for all the pain, the lack, and the loss he had caused them. James recalls, "Mr. Baker just looked at me and said, 'I forgive you, son.'"

"When I hugged him, Vera's dad began to sob," James recalled. "I had to hold that man as he wept. I never, ever experienced somebody weeping so deeply in my entire life. I physically had to hold him up. After a few minutes, he finally got his composure. I went over to Mrs. Baker and asked her the same thing."

For Bert it took a bit longer, but he finally realized that his anger was destroying him from the inside. Finally, he too agreed to forgive James Leggett. Forgive him, yes. Meet him—NO.

But in late 2007, Bert Baker and James Leggett wound up on the same Kairos Prison Ministry team at Palatka Florida's Putnam Correctional Institution, Leggett's former prison. It would be their first meeting in twenty-three years. Some of the other members of the ministry team were concerned that things would not go well or may even get out of hand.

"I saw James when he came into the room," Bert remembered. "He recognized me, and he just stopped in his tracks and hung his head. I walked up to him and said, 'It's been a long time coming.' He looked up at me and said, 'Sure has.' Then my heart just burst. We both just started hugging and crying."

That is a story of forgiveness!

I remember sitting in my church, listening to James and Bert share their story, each one telling his side without giving away the fact that they were telling the same story until the very end. Tears streamed down my face, as the realization of what I was hearing dawned upon me.

I sat transfixed as Bert extended his hand toward the front row, and James Leggett joined him on the platform. As he did, Bert walked over to him and placed his arm across James' shoulder. Bert said, "I have TRULY forgiven James for what has happened, and the Lord has just blessed us both with the fact that we are past this and that we can show love for each other."

Then Bert paused for a moment, as he looked out upon the congregation gathered in front of him. His next words cut us all to the heart. He simply said, "This is my friend, James Leggett."

As we in the Church begin to consider a path forward to implement Christ's command that we *must* love one another, we're going to be faced with many issues of forgiveness. After all, since we've been such a "hostile and disputatious" group, we've all been on the giving AND on the receiving end of offenses (real and imagined), injuries, hurts, and breakups. So, in order to prepare our hearts for what must come, I wanted to share one of the most powerful testimonies of forgiveness I know.[152]

Vera Baker's story is a poignant reminder that the love of Christ can overcome any sin, any offense. The Bakers and the Leggetts are no longer prisoners of their hatred.

---

[152] You can see Bert Baker and James Leggett share their story of forgiveness and freedom at https://www.youtube.com/watch?v=P70F9XT1z-w

What about you?

The first words that Vera's dad, Jesse, spoke to Gator Leggett, after he was released from prison, demonstrated the depth of the work that God had done in his heart. "I forgive you, *son.*"

Yes, he actually called the man who had murdered his daughter, "son." That's *true* forgiveness. It flabbergasts me still.

Isn't it high-time we consider all that Jesus has done to purchase our salvation? When are we going to say, "We've been angry long enough. It is time to get rid of our anger. It is time to honor *His* memory."

Jesus knows that true forgiveness is a necessary ingredient to love and unity. Perhaps that's why He made our receiving forgiveness conditional on our willingness to give it. Christ said, "If you forgive others for their transgressions, your heavenly Father will also forgive you. But if you do not forgive others, then your Father will not forgive your transgressions."[153]

Some versions use the word "sin," instead of transgression. Others use trespass, offense, failure, wrongdoing, or even faults. No matter what you call it when your brother or sister in Christ hasn't lived up to *your* standard, Christ makes the choice He's left you very clear. If you want to be forgiven, then you must forgive. There's no middle ground—forgive or forget the deal.

C. S. Lewis observed, "We all want progress, but if you're on the wrong road, progress means doing an about-turn and walking back to the right road; in that case, the man who turns back soonest is the most progressive."

The path forward to forgiveness, unity, and love is simple.

It's just not easy.

The path I speak of begins at the cross. We need to recognize the place of our own forgiveness. Christ's death on the cross has purchased total and absolute forgiveness from every sin we ever have committed or ever will commit. When we accept the salvation He offers us from the cross, the total price for every sin that ever has or ever will enter our life is fully paid.

During the 2015 Christmas season, an unnamed man would periodically pop into the BP gas station in Otaki, New Zealand, pick random motorists and pay for their fuel purchase. He said, "I'm a Christian and, to

---
[153] Matthew 6:14-15 (NASB)

me, that's what Christmas is about—Jesus giving the ultimate gift."

Just like those motorists, our price has been fully paid. We are forgiven, and some of us are just as surprised as the motorists to find out that Jesus calls us to walk in that forgiveness and to extend it to others. He offers us forgiveness, but also demands that we:

DETERMINE TO FORGIVE

Once the motorist's bill had been paid, of course, the gas station workers in Otaki, New Zealand, never tried to collect additional payment from the folks who had just filled their tanks. It would have been wrong and unfair to ask for payment of the same bill twice just because the payment would be coming from someone else. Not to mention, it would be illegal.

But a willingness to forgive is a required trait of the follower of Christ. Remember Peter's struggle with this? He asked Jesus, "Lord, how often should I forgive someone who sins against me? Seven times?"[154] If someone *deliberately* sinned against you, time after time, after time, I think you'd likely agree that forgiving seven times seems to be a generous standard. But Christ sees it quite differently. His answer to Peter was, "No, not seven times," Jesus replied, "but seventy times seven!"[155] Without Christ, that level of true forgiveness is beyond our capacity!

Perhaps it was for that reason that Christ insisted His disciples remain in Jerusalem until they had received the promise from the Father. Or maybe that's why He poured out His Spirit on Cornelius in front of Peter and the group from Joppa. He knew that if these men were ever going to be able to forgive the past and start walking in love, they would need the fruit of the Holy Spirit.

We have a tendency to sanitize the pages of Scripture as we read them. When we read, for example, about Cornelius being a centurion, we forget the back story to his position in the Roman army. When the emperor sent his troops to rule over a dominated people, he wasn't sending a bunch of boy scouts. The military Rome established, when it created the world's first standing army, was one of the most vicious, well-organized armed forces known to man. By the time General Pompey and his army entered

---

[154] Matthew 18:21 (NLT)
[155] Matthew 18:22 (NLT)

Jerusalem in 63 BC, Rome already ruled most of the Mediterranean region.

The Romans believed that they were sons of Mars, the Roman god of war. The army was a highly organized fighting machine, utterly predatory and bent on domination. It ruled over the territories it conquered with a brutal, iron fist. Peter and the men from Joppa would have had much to forgive.

We, too, have to recognize that any debt we want to collect from someone who has injured or offended us has already been paid by Someone Else. Their failures, faults, and sins have all been paid for already. In fact, they were more than paid. We have no more right to demand payment from them again than the gas station workers did!

The Holy Spirit knew that our willingness to forgive would be a major issue in our lives. That's why we are told in 1 Corinthians 13 that love keeps no record of wrongs. When we keep reminding ourselves of past hurts and pains, we cannot let go and forgive. If we choose to hold onto the list of offenses and sins that someone has perpetrated against us, have we not begun to delight in evil? Paul said that "love does not delight in evil but rejoices with the truth."[156] When we keep a list of those who have sinned against us, we feel that it gives us license to keep the walls up, instead of building bridges. When we keep a record, it provokes us to anger. When we see the debt as paid, we have no grounds for our anger.

Christ deliberately made the Father's offer of forgiveness to us absolutely conditional upon our willingness to accept the same payment He accepts. The blood of Jesus *is* sufficient. The blood of Christ paid the price for *all* sin. "But if you do *not* forgive others," Jesus warns, "your Father will not forgive you." If that price is enough for the Almighty, it has to be enough for you as well. And if you think that you have been so wronged by someone that Christ's sacrifice is NOT enough of a price, you've totally missed it. It IS enough. There is no greater price that could be paid by anyone anywhere.

So God says, "Forgive—or our deal is off."

He really meant it when He taught us to pray, "Forgive us our sins, for we also forgive everyone who sins against us."[157] Think about it. You're

---
[156] 1 Corinthians 13:6
[157] Luke 11:4

asking God to forgive you *because* you also forgive *everyone* who sins against you. *Do you?* If you are holding onto someone's sin, don't be fooled—it is holding onto you, too. Sin always brings pain and death. But an amazing outpouring of grace is available to you when you decide to forgive as you have been forgiven. There is freedom in forgiveness. Just ask Bert Baker!

When we determine to forgive on the basis of Christ's sacrifice, we declare that His Blood is enough for us. Like Vera's father, we can choose to say, "I've been angry long enough." But how can we dare to demand that the price be paid twice? By what standard do we say we will only be satisfied with the Blood of Jesus *and* something else?

Among all of the people who will read this book, thankfully there will not be many who have had a beloved member of their family brutally murdered, though sadly there will be some. Most of us will have offenses to forgive that are much, much smaller. But there is no offense, no sin so great that is was not paid for at the cross. The lesson the Bakers have demonstrated is this: Even when someone has taken the life of your daughter or your sister, the love of Christ can bring you to a place of total freedom and lead you to absolute forgiveness for the person who offended you.

That's great news, to be sure. But as Bert found out, forgiveness is only a great beginning. It isn't enough that we determine to forgive, we must also:

DETERMINE TO LOVE

Loving one another is the only instruction that Christ left for us and called it a *commandment*. It was clearly important to Him. So important, in fact, that He even qualified His words: "A new command I give you: Love one another. As I have loved you, so you must love one another. By this everyone will know that you are My disciples, if you love one another."[158] It wasn't enough that we love one another by a standard that *we* chose, but we have to love one another *as He has loved us*!

Frankly, that's a much higher standard than I would set. If it were up to me, I'd probably say something like, "Sure I want you to love one

---
[158] John 13:34-35

another, but I know how tough that is. So give it your best shot. You know, just try really, really hard. But if it doesn't work out, what can you do?" But that wasn't the plan Jesus left for us. He knew that it would take nothing less than us choosing to love others the way He had loved us, if we were to have the kind of unity He envisioned for His Body. So He set the standard very high. So impossibly high, in fact, that unless His Spirit is living and working in us, the task is totally impossible.

Love is the central element in the Christian walk. It is the critical identifying factor of true Christianity. Your faith is important, that is true. But no matter what your faith leads you to do, you're wasting your efforts unless they are founded upon love. Deep, insightful prophecies without love are worthless. Amazing faith, with incredible manifestations, is meaningless without love. Taking a vow of poverty and living in a cave will profit you nothing unless you have love.

> No matter what your faith leads you to do, you're wasting your efforts unless they are founded upon love.

Paul said it this way. "The only thing that counts is faith expressing itself through love."[159] It is the *only thing* that counts. Faith isn't enough. People can't see into your heart and mind to know what you believe. Faith must be acted upon in order to be seen by others. When they see your faith, it had better be an expression of the love of Christ inside you. It must be faith that expresses His love and draws them to a relationship with Him, because He is their only hope for salvation. If it is not, then it doesn't really matter what you do. If what Paul wrote in 1 Corinthians 13 is true (and we know it is), then it will profit you nothing without love.

Love is the greatest weapon in our arsenal!

Saeed Abedini is an Iranian-American pastor who used to regularly travel back to his birth country to help establish churches and orphanages and to encourage Christians there. Abedini was imprisoned in Iran in 2012 for setting up home churches in the Islamic nation and charged with compromising national security. Pastor Saeed sat in the prisons of Iran for more than three years, regularly beaten and tortured, often refused even

---

[159] Galatians 5:6

clothes to cover his body. In my role with the American Center for Law & Justice, I played a small part in working for his eventual release in January of 2016.

The day that he was to be released, he stood blindfolded under guard in a small room. When a man standing next to Pastor Saeed spoke, he heard the voice of the man who had brutally beaten him during the years of torture, aimed at forcing him to recant his faith.

On the first day of his imprisonment, that man had made numerous threats against Pastor Saeed. But Saeed had told him, "Whatever you do to me, still on the last day that I see you, I am going to hug you and tell you that I love you. You can never push hate into my heart." For three and a half years, this brute tortured Pastor Saeed.

But standing in that room just two hours before a plane would take him from Iran to freedom, Pastor Saeed recognized his captor's voice, reached out and grabbed his interrogator's hand. He pulled the man to him and hugged him. As he did, his former captor began to shake and gave him permission to remove his blindfold.

"Do you remember what I told you on the first day we met?" Pastor Saeed asked him.

"No, I don't remember," the man replied, but his eyes betrayed his lie.

The pastor's voice spoke softly as he said, "I remember. I told you that you could never make me hate you. I told you that the love Jesus placed inside of me would allow me to forgive you, day after day, and would allow me to love you. You know I have been praying for you. I want to tell you now that I forgive you for all that you have done to me. I love you."

Pastor Saeed had determined to forgive. He had decided in advance that he would love. His decision to love, in spite of abuse and torture, gave him the victory and glorified the name of Jesus.

Make no mistake, our refusal to love one another in the Body of Christ is *sin*. Despite Christ's clear admonition that our refusal to forgive will affect the forgiveness He is willing to offer us, we choose to withhold grace. And in the face of a direct command from our Lord to love one another as He loved us, we refuse to repent. Pastor Saeed was determined to continue in love, even for a man who tortured him. We're determined to withhold communion from someone Christ has accepted into His Body because they hold some different understandings than we do. You tell me which one is truly displaying the love of Christ?

Love is the ultimate expression of the outworking of the Holy Spirit in us. Do you think it's just a coincidence that the first fruit of the Spirit Paul lists in Galatians 5:22 is LOVE?

We've forgotten that love is a *verb*, not just a noun. Its expressions are actions, lived out in the day-to-day lives we lead in this world. Those actions must be an expression of the love of Christ or they miss the mark. No matter what else we do for the Kingdom of God, unless it is founded upon, characterized by, and empowered with the love of Christ—it is worthless.

We cannot get around the fact that Christ commanded us to love one another. His command is central to the success of our mission.

Have you ever considered the things that Christ never presented to us as a command? Of course, the instruction in Matthew 28:19 to "go into all the world and make disciples" is an imperative. But Christ never said, "Here's another new command I have for you, go into all the world..." When He told His disciples to let their light shine before men in Matthew 5:16, Jesus never prefaced that with, "And here's an important command for you to obey." Not even when giving us the signal expression of our unity with Him did Christ say, "Here is my final command, do this in remembrance of Me."

These are not insignificant items. The Great Commission is critical to the preaching of the gospel. At the very least, the Lord's Table is central to our identification with Him. To many of us, it is so much more than that. But Jesus didn't wrap these in the language of a command, as He did with His command to "love one another as I have loved you."

Isn't the reason obvious? We can invest millions of dollars and thousands of lives to go into the entire world and preach the gospel, but if the way we love one another does not compel the world to recognize we are disciples of Jesus Christ, all we are doing is propagating our own prejudice. Christ's warning in this instance is scary and severe: "Woe to you, teachers of the law and Pharisees, you hypocrites! You travel over land and sea to win a single convert, and when he becomes one, you make him twice as much a son of hell as you are."[160]

If we teach our converts that our particular brand of Christianity, our choices for worship style or governance are the only true way, then are we not undermining His command to love one another? Don't we infect our followers with sinful pride by making the claim that "we are the (insert your denomination name here) church and we have the truth!"?

Interestingly, in 1 Corinthians 13, Paul tells us that one of the characteristics of love is that love "does not insist on its own way."[161] True love, intrinsically, recognizes that there may be other valid and righteous expressions of love. Because love is patient and kind, it can continue to love, while the one being loved grows in his maturity. True love between Christians would neither envy the growth of a different denomination, nor boast of its own growth. The love that Paul envisions would never rudely accuse another believer of hateful heresies simply because they hold a different view of when or how to baptize someone, or because they dress differently.

About 130 years ago, the House of Bishops of the Protestant Episcopal Church met in Chicago. One of the main issues on the table was that of church unity. Out of that meeting, came a document called the Chicago-Lambeth Quadrilateral,[162] since it focused on four necessary points as the basis of Christian unity. They made it clear they wanted to see John 17 fulfilled in their day in as deep and true a manner as possible.

In a striking example of a love that "does not insist on its own way,"[163] they promised that "in all things of human ordering or human choice, relating to modes of worship and discipline, or to traditional customs, this Church is ready, in the spirit of love and humility, to forego all preferences of her own." In other words, they did not insist their way was right or even best. Their main goal was unity in diversity. These bishops offered to accept and receive the practices of other true believers in Jesus if it would bring about the love that Christ called us to.

Uniformity was not their intent. They were *not* trying to create one

---

[160] Matthew 23:15
[161] 1 Corinthians 13:5 (ESV)
[162] http://anglicansonline.org/basics/Chicago_Lambeth.html
[163] 1 Corinthians 13:5 (ESV)

huge super-denomination. They wrote, "This Church does not seek to absorb other Communions, but rather, co-operating with them on the basis of a common Faith and Order, to discountenance schism, to heal the wounds of the Body of Christ, and to promote the charity [today we'd call that love] which is the chief of Christian graces and the visible manifestation of Christ to the world." Cooperation. What a marvelous concept.

Love always seeks relationship, someone with whom to share the love within. This is the essence of the Great Commission. We are charged with reaching out and sharing God's love with the world. If our message is to be effective and if we are to be known as Christ's disciples, then we need to be characterized as a people of love. We must seek out opportunities to build bridges with other believers, encourage them to forgive, and help them to develop a life characterized by love. This will demand that we work outside of our comfort zone.

Don't you think that Jesus had a difficult time with prostitutes and thieves? There was an element of holiness in His character that had to be rebuffed by their sin. But His desire to engage them in the love of God allowed Him to overcome that. They may not have been all that they would become. But He still loved them.

---✛---

Love wins. It wins over hatred. It wins over sin.
It wins over faith that is too weak to be effective.

Paul instructs us to "accept the one whose faith is weak, without quarreling over disputable matters."[164] The only way we can build up our brother is to be in a relationship with him. If we begin our relationship by arguing and quarreling about the things that are different between us, we'll never get to the important things. Growing in our faith is an important thing. Learning to display the love of Christ is an important thing. Again, these are the "disputable matters," not the issues of sin we discussed previously.

We are called to please Christ by making "every effort to do what

---

[164] Romans 14:1

leads to peace and to mutual edification."[165] "Every effort"—that's a pretty inclusive phrase. Ask yourself "Am I making *every effort* to build relationships that lead to peace and mutual edification with other believers?" For most of us, the arrow will fall far short of the mark.

For many of us in the modern world, we find ourselves surrounded by things that consume our time. Between our cell phones, the Internet, game consoles, and cable television, we hardly have enough time for our family. Even the way we entertain ourselves has shifted. For many families, everyone watches TV or plays their games in a separate place. Making every effort to build relationships will require a change in our attitude and our outlook.

Do Hard Things: A Teenage Rebellion Against Low Expectations is a popular Christian book authored by Alex and Brett Harris. Written by eighteen-year-old twins, the book challenges teenagers to go beyond their comfort zone and take personal responsibility to "do hard things." In their book, Alex and Brett show that, prior to the 20th century, a person was either an adult or a child. After leaving childhood, people WORKED and had responsibilities. Being a teenager is a modern development that has become characterized by low expectations.

The Church has become like a teenager, don't you think? It used to be that the Church was like the army of God, marching forth in faith determined to proclaim the message. Nothing was going to stop them. They were determined to strive, side-by-side, for the sake of the gospel. Nothing could scare them. Nothing could get them to quit.

Nowadays, the Church is more like a Cub Scout pack. (No offense intended to the Cub Scouts.) We get together on a regular basis for fun, fellowship, and activities which are ostensibly teaching us things. Except that the things we are learning don't typically impact the way we live our daily lives. It's fun, but not world changing. I comment in the chapter "Discerning the Body," that the original church was unstoppable in its unity. Well, in our current state of fighting one another, we are not very unstoppable now, are we?

We've set the bar so low that we expect almost nothing of someone who wants to claim the name of "Christian." According to articles I have

---

[165] Romans 14:19

read online, we can expect them to come twice a month, if we keep the services to about an hour and fifteen minutes. That's IF they like the music AND good childcare is provided, AND if no one else comes who they don't get along with, AND if the preacher doesn't offend them. A nice café in the foyer with excellent free coffee doesn't hurt, either! If we do this, then we can expect the semi-regular involvement of people who want to call themselves followers of Christ.

REALLY? FOLLOWERS OF CHRIST? Is this the same Jesus we've been discussing? As I recall, He said something about dying to self and taking up our cross, not pampering ourselves and sipping a mocha latte.

We spent a lot of time together in Chapter three looking at Philippians 1:27-28. We spoke about "conducting ourselves in a manner worthy of the gospel of Christ." We cannot possibly do that without forgiving one another and determining to walk in love, striving with one another and contending as one man for the faith. Instead, we have become content striving against one another. That's not even close to the same thing.

Striving *together* takes a real effort. It is too easy to be at home by ourselves, entertained by our devices. Building and maintaining relationships requires a time investment. And for those who consider themselves the "stronger" and "more mature" Christians, we are called to reach out to those who are weaker and strengthen them in the faith. Paul says, "We who are strong ought to bear with the failings of the weak and not to please ourselves. Each of us should please his neighbor for his good, to build him up."[166]

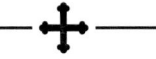

> The life of love lived by the early church compelled the world to take notice.

The Body of Christ must build itself up in love. Only as we are equipped and strengthened will we be able to demonstrate the love that is to characterize us as disciples. Only then will we be the witness that the world cannot ignore. Only then will we become, once again, the unstoppable Body of Christ. The life of love lived by the early church compelled the world to take notice. Some took notice and opposed them, others joined them; but everyone noticed!

---
[166] Romans 15:1–2 (NASB)

COUNT TO ONE

Christ gave us our leaders, those called and gifted to equip us and train us, to bring us to the point where we "all attain to the unity of the faith, and of the knowledge of the Son of God, to a mature man, to the measure of the stature which belongs to the fullness of Christ."[167] Our knowledge and our maturity are intended to lead us to the unity of the faith. *The* faith! The *One* Body! Paul gives us the outcome.

> As a result, we are no longer to be children, tossed here and there by waves and carried about by every wind of doctrine, by the trickery of men, by craftiness in deceitful scheming; but speaking the truth in love, we are to grow up in all aspects into Him who is the head, even Christ, from whom the whole body, being fitted and held together by what every joint supplies, according to the proper working of each individual part, causes the growth of the body for the building up of itself in love.[168]

"The whole body building itself up in love"—as we do, the schemes of the enemy and the lies of the world won't be able to divide us. Fitted together by what we supply to one another, walking together in deliberately loving relationships with one another, we'll learn that each part works well with the other. And the Body of Christ grows. Doctrinal differences on disputable matters won't divide us, because we understand that we are designed to be different. It is all about being bound together in the love of Christ as ONE BODY.

Bert Baker can sit in front of anybody in the world and speak on the power of forgiveness and love. If he's sitting next to James Leggett, their story is even more compelling. Why? Because Bert and James are living out the one command that Christ left us, they love one another as He loved them—totally, fully, selflessly. And the power that brings to their testimony is awesome!

Bert and James have learned that the mission to be an ambassador for Christ is more important than anything else. Even the murder of Vera Baker is utterly overcome by the murder of Jesus Christ. Their love for

---

[167] Ephesians 4:13
[168] Ephesians 4:14-16 (NASB)

Christ compels them. They are *really living like* people who are convinced that since One died for all, they *cannot* live for themselves nor for their petty interests any longer. They must live for Him Who died for them and was raised again. (You know, like the apostle Paul wrote in 2 Corinthians 5:14.) A life controlled by radical love and characterized by a willingness to forgive and work together for the sake of the gospel is unstoppable.

To paraphrase C.S. Lewis, aim at walking in the love of Christ and you get unity thrown in. Aim at unity for unity's sake and you get neither. And as we walk in the love of Christ, we will become again what we were created to be, the unstoppable Body of Christ.

We must become one body again. If we won't, then we have effectively decided to abandon the mission.

I close with a prayer adapted from the *Book of Common Prayer*:

Gracious Father, we pray for Thy one, holy, catholic and apostolic Church that is the one Body of Christ, composed of all who have been placed in Christ by grace through faith in His Name. Fill it with all truth, in all truth with all peace. Where it is corrupt, purify it; where it is in error, correct it; where in anything it is amiss, reform it. Where it is right, strengthen it; where it is in want, provide for it; where it is divided, reunite it; for the sake of Jesus Christ Thy Son our Savior. Amen.[169]

Together.
Unstoppable.
One Body.

By learning to forgive with all our hearts and walk in His love, we will have learned to *Count to One*.

---

[169] Adapted from the *Book of Common Prayer*.

Epilogue

DEALING WITH DISCIPLINE

As we have seen, there comes a time when the Bible demands that one party stand apart from the other. This is not a light decision, nor can it ever be an easy one. But in order for the separation to be biblical in its process, both the decision and the process must be characterized by whole-hearted, unconditional love.

This appears to be a contradiction, doesn't it? How can you induce a deliberate separation on the basis of unconditional love? How exactly does one expel someone from a close community *in love?* To answer that question, I will share a painful letter that Joe, a man I know, was forced to write his son.

Joe's son Kevin was a young man in his early twenties who had been raised in a Christian family, but he had been pulling further and further away from Christ. Driven by sinful desires which had taken a controlling position in his life, Kevin went from being trustworthy and reliable to someone who was frequently caught lying as he tried to live a double life. After months of trying to help his son work through issues of choices, responsibility, character, and personal accountability, Joe and his wife realized the time had come to insist on a choice. Joe had to demand the same thing of Kevin that Elijah had demanded of the people of Israel in 1 Kings 18: "How long will you waver between two opinions? If the Lord is God, follow Him; but if Baal is God, follow him."

Sadly, Kevin decided to move out of the family home and move in with his girlfriend. Joe's letter to his son exhibits precisely the elements needed when a separation is demanded—firmness, consistency of character, a willingness to forgive, a deep desire for restoration, and—most importantly—unbridled, unconditional love.

Here is the letter he wrote to his son:

Dear Kevin,

This is the letter that I hoped to never have to write to you.

As we've walked together through the years, we've faced and overcome many difficult challenges. As a family, we've always been able to stand together, fight together and enjoy the victory together. We have sought the counsel and direction of the Lord as a family, and enjoyed His blessing and provision even in the most difficult of times. We've never let anything come between us, and we've been the stronger for it.

Now you have decided to abandon that.

I know that you believe your choice to move in with your girlfriend will bring you joy, but it will not. For sure it will bring you pleasure for a time—but pleasure and joy are two very different things. Sadly, soon the pleasure will begin to fade and the reality of the circumstances in which you have placed yourself will become all too real. When sex ceases to be a servant it becomes a very cruel master. And as the character you've built over the years continues to unravel, your life will do so, too. You are headed for a very painful place.

When the day comes—and come it will—that you recognize the folly of your choices, I want you to remember that you have a loving family that truly cares for you. Mom and I will always be here for you until the day we die. Our love for you is an unconditional one; it is not based upon

> Our love for you is an unconditional one; it is not based upon your choices, but upon ours.

your choices, but upon ours. We choose to love you. I also want to remind you that God, too, loves you with an unconditional love, and He has promised never to leave you or forsake you. He, too, is longing for the day that you choose to return to Him. He, too, will welcome you with open arms when you choose to return to Him. Luke 15:11-32 is the story of the father waiting for his prodigal son to return home; just as I am waiting for you.

But beware of the horrifying fact that God will allow you to draw away, because true love cannot be forced. He will allow your heart to grow cold. He will never forsake you, but YOU can choose to abandon Him. And should you do so, an eternity of unspeakable pain awaits you. Hell is not a wise choice for anyone to make, least of all one who knows better and has tasted the joys of serving a loving and merciful God. Forever is a very, very long time indeed.

Let me speak for a moment from my heart. You've observed my character for your entire life. You've watched how I live my life, make my choices, care for my family, serve my God. You've seen how I sacrifice to provide for you and your sister, and how I've lived a life that you have always wanted to emulate. Let the years speak to your heart, son; and ask yourself if the choices you're making now will lead you to become the kind of man you've admired, the kind of man you've always wanted to be. Are you living the example you'd want YOUR SONS to follow? Are you making decisions based on principles that have led real men for ages?

You and I both know the answer. This is not a decision you will look back on with pride. This is not something you'll share with your sons and daughters and encourage them to emulate.

Forcing you to choose between your lifestyle and your heritage has been one of the most difficult decisions in my life. But I love you far too much to participate in your destruction, to provide the provision for the suicide of your integrity. You know my heart, and you know that I have walked this process with you for months, all the while begging you to consider who you truly want to be as a man. For months I've felt that you were slipping farther and farther away, and did everything I could to help you see it also.

But I finally came to the place where I could not walk with you any further down the path you have chosen. I am convinced that not to require this choice from you would be more detrimental to you, to your sister and to our family. Always remember that it was your choice, not mine, to leave the family home in this manner. Also, please always remember that it will be your choice when to return home. I look forward to the day when I can once again help you to accomplish your goals, once again participate in your plans, once again truly share my life with you. When you choose to turn around you will always have a father waiting for you with open arms. Please carefully consider this—it is not too late to turn around. Now. You don't have to follow through on your decision to move out if you make the right choices. You can turn around today, instead of waiting days, weeks, months or years. It doesn't have to be later, it can be today.

However, if you do not choose to turn around now, I do hope that, in the interim, you will choose to remain involved with the family. You know that we gather here at home on Sunday afternoons. We eat lunch, play games together, hang out and talk. You and Monica are welcome to join us, just call and let us know when/if you choose to do so. You're both also welcome to be a part of our family's celebrations and holidays (such as Thanksgiving and Christmas), if you let us know in advance so

---

> When you choose to turn around you will always have a father waiting for you with open arms.

we can make plans to include you. If there are other times that you'd like to come over and visit, just let us know; we'd love to see you and will coordinate a mutually convenient time.

Finally, let me share the impact I have felt in this. I need you to know that your choices have made me feel something for you that I have never felt before—shame. I am ashamed of you. That is something I have never had to say before, something I had hoped never to have to say at all. But I needed you to know.

Your choices have broken my heart, and I feel hurt in ways I never imagined possible. You are not the man I raised you to be. You've chosen to abandon everything I taught you about being a man of character. I feel betrayed. I don't say this to hurt you, but to let you know my true feelings. I do this because I have always been honest with you, and always trusted you to be honest with me. Our discussions over the past few weeks have made it clear that you've decided not to continue that precedent, but I have not and will not abandon it.

But having said that, do not hear that I am closing the door; for as I have said very clearly, our door is always open to you when you choose to turn around. But I love you too much not to be honest with you about the impact of what you've done.

Finally, I want to remind you that I do love you. I have had to say some very hard things to you in this letter, son; but you needed to hear them. But most of all, always remember that I love you.

Love, Dad

As you can see from reading his letter, it broke Joe's heart to have to write it. Everything within him wanted to be able to keep the close relationship he had developed with his son. But the overriding issue was not his son but *sin*. Sin was driving a wedge into the relationship which could not be ignored. To allow it to continue unaddressed would undermine the foundation of Christian grace and truth in the family.

Joe's letter illustrated several excellent and necessary elements that characterize a love-driven separation. Here are the main ones I see.

We've been one

Joe began his letter by reaffirming that his heart was for unity, not division. "This is the letter I hoped never to have to write to you." Joe was expressing that nothing would mean more to him than *not* having to write this way to his son, but Joe's love for his son compelled him to do so.

He also reminded Kevin that they had been one family. "We've walked together…we've always been able to stand together…we've never let anything come between us." These are appeals to historic unity, a reminder that the past difficulties were never enough to bring separation. In so doing, Joe is appealing to Kevin's memory of how they have faced battles together in the past. The key word is "together"—they have fought as one.

Share God's wisdom

Joe then shares God's wisdom. He shares principles from God's Word, without sharing chapter and verse. He knows that Kevin will very likely be able to recall the passages his Dad is referring to, there's no need to become overbearing, and Joe gently reminds his son of the truth.

Share God's welcoming heart

God is a God of restoration. He is anxious to forgive and to welcome us back. This is the lesson we see in the parable of the prodigal son. The father was looking for his son, rejoiced in his repentance, and celebrated his return. Joe expresses these both from the standpoint of God's willingness to welcome Kevin's repentance, as well as his own determination to forgive when the time to do so presents itself.

Share God's warnings

But there are two sides to this issue. On the one hand, God will welcome Kevin back when he repents and abandons his sin. On the other hand, God will *not* force Kevin in to a love relationship with Him. Joe warns Kevin the road he is walking ends at a cliff. It is all too easy to walk too far before you realize the ground is no longer under your feet.

Appeal to history, truth, and logic

Joe also appeals to the example of the life he has lived before his son, a life his son had previously admired. Kevin has benefited from Joe's choices. Joe begs his son to "let the years speak to [his] heart," and to examine the long-term impact of his choices. Joe is saying, "You know better than this. Think it through."

Show a commitment to what is best

Joe demonstrated that he is committed to what is best—*really* best—for everyone involved. He says, "I love you too much to participate in your destruction." He reminds Kevin that he has been working with him for months and months to try to resolve these issues. Even that process demonstrates Joe's commitment to what is best for everyone.

Appeal for reconsideration

Ultimately, this is Kevin's decision, and he must make it. So Joe appeals to him. "Please carefully reconsider this—it is not too late to turn around. Now." Kevin can change the outcome by changing his direction. Repentance is "turning around" and deciding to walk TO God and WITH God, instead of away from Him. Since this is a decision that Kevin must make on his own, Joe appeals for him to reconsider, if not today, then tomorrow.

Maintain communication

Joe makes it clear that he is not closing the door on communication, nor terminating their relationship. Joe knows that every involvement with he and his wife, and each interaction with the family, is another chance for

God to draw Kevin back to a place of wholeness. Even Monica is welcome. Joe is willing to put his personal pain aside in the short-term in order to have a chance to influence the situation in the long-term.

SHARE THE PAIN

Joe makes it very clear to Kevin that his choices are causing deep pain. He neither attacks nor brow-beats his son, but he does make it clear that Kevin's sin has broken his father's heart. This, too, is an appeal from the foundation of love. Through the pain, Joe stands determined to reach out for restoration.

KEEP THE DOOR FOR COMMUNICATION OPEN

Joe makes it clear that the offer of reconciliation remains. "Our door is always open to you..." But he also reiterates the price of admission, "...when you choose to turn around." Sinners are always welcomed, sin always rejected. Christian families are to be places of ongoing and continual forgiveness. And the Church is just another Christian family.

REAFFIRM THE BASIS OF LOVE

The final message Joe leaves with Kevin is a reaffirmation of his deep and abiding love.

This, then, is how a community of faith (whether it is a family or a church) reacts when sin demands distance. It is *never* intended as permanent, because God *always* stands ready to forgive when a sinner repents.

As believers, men and women who claim the name of Jesus, we are called to exhibit His same characteristics. We must appeal to unity, share God's wisdom, His welcoming heart and His warnings—each of them is an expression of the Father's deep love. We can appeal to our history to draw the heart of the sinner back to the ones who love him. We are called to be committed to the highest good and appeal to the errant person to reconsider what he is choosing to do.

Most of all, we must make sure that we always leave the door open for the repentant to return. The lesson from the parable of the prodigal is not just that the father rejoices at the return of the son. It is also that we are to express the heart of the father, not that of the brother.

Restoration. Reunification.

It's the heartbeat of the Father.

Questions For
Individual
Study
and
Reflection

Before We Begin: The Groundwork

1. What barriers to unity are created by my personal history?

   _____

   _____

   _____

   _____

   _____

2. Are there specific areas of pain or unforgiveness I need the Lord to heal, so that I can move forward into a greater unity with the Body of Christ?

   _____

   _____

   _____

   _____

   _____

3. Am I holding on to specific prejudices against a particular race, group, or denomination that would hinder developing a good relationship with them?

   _____

   _____

   _____

   _____

   _____

Chapter 1:

REFLECTIONS ON CHRISTIAN UNITY

1. Would I have been comfortable worshipping with the diverse group of people gathered in Jerusalem in 2015? Why or why not?

2. What is my reaction to the "love God above all, and love others" suggestion as a guide for Christian relations?

3. After comparing my response above to Jesus' words in Matthew 22:37-39, do I need to reconsider my initial answer?

Chapter 2:

"I Hear There Are Divisions Among You"

1. Aside from my sin, what are some of the other barriers to true unity I see? How can these be overcome?

   _____
   _____
   _____
   _____
   _____

2. Do I believe that Jesus would welcome a truly saved person from a different denomination to His communion table?

   _____
   _____
   _____
   _____
   _____

3. What specific action can I take this week to begin to develop a greater heart for Christian unity and be reconciled to other believers?

   _____
   _____
   _____
   _____
   _____

Chapter 3:
DISCERNING THE BODY

1. What are my thoughts regarding the three historic streams of Christianity? Which have been a normative part of my faith experience and which have not?

2. How would my personal faith likely be impacted by experiencing the streams I do not currently embrace?

3. What gifts have I been given to serve God? What gifts do I need in others to complete me and make me more effective?

Chapter 4:

In Christ

1. How has my understanding of faith and doctrine grown since I have come to Christ? Do I believe that my understanding is perfect now?

   _____
   _____
   _____
   _____
   _____

2. As I try recalling the time I came to Christ by faith in His work on the cross alone, is it clear to me that I have definitely made that choice for my own life? (If not, then might I suggest you take a look at the final section of the book, called: "How Can I Be Sure I Know Jesus?")

   _____
   _____
   _____
   _____
   _____

Chapter 5:
HISTORICAL FOUNDATIONS

1. How does my personal faith agree with the Nicene Creed?

2. How does it differ?

3. Are the areas where my personal faith differs from the Nicene Creed based upon my understanding of Scripture or something else?

Chapter 6:
Unity—Not Uniformity

1. Have I "thrown away" any groups of Christians just because they are different from me?

2. Do I truly believe that John 3:16 really applies to "whoever believes?"

3. What can I do this week to deliberately build a relationship with a believer from a group I have pushed away?

QUESTIONS FOR INDIVIDUAL STUDY AND REFLECTION

Chapter 7:

UNITY—NOT UNIFICATION

1. Have I clearly defined my personal "faith essentials?" If so, what are they? What Scriptures are they based upon?

2. What does the Nicene Creed show about the important elements of Christ's character?

3. Read the answer to the question, "Who is the one true Church?" on page 121? Do you agree? If not, what is the basis for your disagreement?

Chapter 8:
FOR THE SAKE OF THE GLORY

1. What elements do I see as necessary to "proper worship?" How much of that viewpoint is based upon my personal experience or personal preference?

2. As I look back on my life for the past week, how has my faith been clearly expressed through love?

3. How can I deliberately draw into a greater unity with Christ in order to display the Father's glory?

Chapter 9:
DEALING WITH THE DIFFERENCES

1. What artificial barriers have I set up that are keeping me away from a better relationship with my brothers and sisters in Christ?

2. Consider my personal role as an ambassador of reconciliation. Who am I in contact with that needs to hear about the message of reconciliation offered by Jesus Christ? How can I reach out to them?

3. How has God specifically gifted me to serve? What are my gifts? Am I using them to advance His Kingdom?

Chapter 10:

A Path Forward

1. Whom do I need to forgive?

2. Am I willing to ask God to work full forgiveness in me for any and every offense?

3. Am I making every effort to maintain the unity of the Spirit in the bonds of peace and to reach out to those who are weaker and strengthen them in their faith?

Questions For Group

Study and Reflection

BEFORE WE BEGIN: THE GROUNDWORK

1. Is our church congregation diverse or is it basically homogeneous?

2. When was the last time that our church participated in an event with believers from other churches in our community? Is that typical behavior for us or extraordinary?

3. What can we do in our local congregation to develop a greater awareness of the unity which Jesus Christ prayed for in John 17?

Chapter 1:

REFLECTIONS ON CHRISTIAN UNITY

1. Discuss the statement: "Knowing Jesus and loving Him was a sufficient basis for us to gather together and praise Him." Would this be seen as a sufficient basis in our church?

2. If our church were to reach out to another group of believers in our area and invite them to a joint time of worship, praise, and prayer, what would it take to make it successful?

Chapter 2:

I Hear There Are Divisions Among You

1. Discuss the "Transformational Essential"—IN CHRIST. What does it mean to be "in Christ?" If someone is truly in Christ, aren't we part of His Body together?

2. What standard does our congregation set to allow a person to join us at the Lord's Table? How does is compare with Scripture?

Chapter 3:

Discerning The Body

1. Which of the three streams are a regular part of our church's worship expression and experience?

2. Are we making every effort to maintain the unity of the Spirit in the bonds of peace? If not, what more could we do?

3. What would real Christian unity look like in our community?

Chapter 4:

IN CHRIST

1. What areas of doctrine have been refined and matured in our congregation or denomination?

2. How does an agreement on the gospel we preach open new doors for cooperative work with other believers in our community?

Chapter 5:

HISTORICAL FOUNDATIONS

1. Review our church or denomination's Statement of Faith. Discuss how our specific congregation reflects the things it contains.

2. How does our church or denomination's Statement of Faith compare to the Nicene Creed?

Chapter 6:

UNITY—NOT UNIFORMITY

1. How does our congregation "score" on the acceptance test?

2. What factors have we historically said determine who is and who is not a Christian? From a scriptural perspective, how valid are they?

3. What traditions do we have that may limit our ability to connect to other believers in Christ?

Chapter 7:

UNITY—NOT UNIFICATION

1. How do we find the balance between holding on to our preferred faith expressions and allowing our brothers and sisters in Christ to do the same?

2. How does the diversity of the Body of Christ help the gospel reach different elements of our community?

3. Read the answer to the question "Who is the one true Church?" on page 121? Does our congregation agree? If not, what is the basis for our disagreement?

QUESTIONS FOR GROUP STUDY AND REFLECTION

Chapter 8:

FOR THE SAKE OF THE GLORY

1. Would outsiders or visitors to our church see our congregation as loving and accepting? Give some specific examples of why or why not.

2. How has the Lord's Prayer impacted the ministry here in our congregation?

3. How can we deliberately make a greater place for the glory of God in our ministry?

Chapter 9:

DEALING WITH THE DIFFERENCES

1. What can we do as a congregation to remove any artificial barriers of separation we have erected?

2. How can our church show the love of Jesus Christ to people trapped in a lifestyle dominated by sin without affirming their sin?

3. Does our congregation deliberately plug people into service areas in which God has gifted them?

Chapter 10:

A Path Forward

1. How can we come together as a congregation and help one another to fully forgive?

2. How can we accept the one whose faith is weak, without quarreling over disputable matters?

How Can I Be Sure I Know Jesus?

The message of the gospel is so simple that even a young child can understand it. And yet, its claims are so astounding that they may be difficult to believe. Coming to know Jesus, really *knowing* Him, rather than just knowing *about* Him, is one of the most significant experiences one can ever have. Read on, and I'll explain why. But more than that, I'll share the best news that anyone has ever heard—*HOW* to be certain you have the relationship with Jesus which He promises in the Bible.

The simple message of the gospel is this:

It is by grace you have been saved, through faith—and this is not from yourselves, it is the gift of God—not by works.[170]

In a nutshell, that is the *what* of the gospel. Let's take a closer look at the key parts of that verse from Ephesians 2 to make sure we understand what God is telling us.

It Is By Grace You Have Been Saved...

Grace is simply something God offers us as a gift. The cost of the gift was totally paid by Jesus Christ and His death on the cross, so there is nothing we can do to add to it or to pay for it. In other words, we are not saved because of anything we have done. It's totally because of what Jesus

---

[170] Ephesians 2:8-9

has done for us. Someone has said that the word *grace* can be thought of as a simple acronym—God's Riches At Christ's Expense. That's pretty clear. It's ALL Jesus. Period.

Through Faith...

When we want to accept God's offer of salvation, we receive it by placing our faith in Jesus Christ. (We'll get to the *how* in just a moment.) But the key thing to understand here is that it is through our faith, not our works. There is nothing we can do to earn our salvation—no amount of good works, prayers, Bible reading, or anything else; only though faith. So God essentially repeats Himself, telling us again that it's ALL Jesus.

This Is Not From Yourselves

This part of the verse simply highlights what the last part says. That's important, because when we see something being repeated in Scripture, it is God's way of drawing our attention to it. It's as though He's saying, "Hey, don't miss this point. It is important!" In this case, God is doing that because the offer made to us seems so amazing, many find it difficult to accept.

Some people feel like they need to do something to be "worthy" of the offer, but there is nothing we can do. God says it is a gift. It is NOT from ourselves. We cannot be good enough, we cannot be nice enough. It makes no difference how terrible our lives have been in the past, because God is reconciling the world to Himself in Christ, not counting our sins against us.

Once again, it's ALL Jesus.

It Is the Gift of God

God is driving the point home. A gift is being given. But like any other gift, it must be received.

If you're keeping count, this is the fourth time God is telling us the same thing.

Not By Works

It is received by faith, *not* by works. As much as we may want to do something to show God we are trying hard to be worthy, there is nothing we can do. And the reason is a simple one, everything that needs to be done has already been done for us by Jesus. Nothing we have to offer can be added to His death on the cross.

When God repeats something FIVE TIMES inside of two verses, you know that He's trying to get your attention and drive home the point He is making. So don't miss His point because of your background, your heritage, your previous understandings, or anything else. There is *nothing* you can do to earn your salvation. It's ALL Jesus. Period.

Now, we move on to the *how* of making sure you have received this incredible gift and truly know Jesus. How can you receive this gift by placing your faith in Him? This, too, is made very clear and simple in the Bible.

First, let me make the point that it applies to everyone equally, whether you have no background in Christianity at all, come from a faith community that baptizes infants as their introduction to the Body of Christ, or come from a faith tradition that sees a profession of faith as the beginning of a new life in Christ. Here's why.

If you come from a Christian community that chooses to baptize infants, all of them also recognize that there comes a point in a person's life when he needs to personally affirm the faith he has been raised in. For example, in the Lutheran church this step of personal profession is called: *confirmation* or *affirmation of baptism.* It is simply a time for each person to publicly profess they have *personally* placed their faith in Christ. Every faith tradition that baptizes infants has a similar practice for their young adults.

If you come from a Christian community that does not practice infant baptism, then it is likely common for people to respond to some sort of an altar call to make a public profession of their faith. This can be done at any point in a person's life, whether they are young or old. Many of these communities have a ceremony of dedication for their young children instead of a baptism.

Regardless, there comes a time in the life of each person who wants to live their life under the name of "Christian" when he is expected to make a personal and public statement of faith, saying: "I have received Jesus Christ as my Lord by faith."

This is a decision we all need to come to personally. The Bible tells us, "All have sinned and fall short of the glory of God."[171] None of us is going to make the grade on our own. We have all violated our conscience. All of us have violated God's righteous standards. So, we need something we cannot possibly get on our own.

We need a Savior, because we also learn from the Bible that "the wages of sin is death."[172] Thankfully, that's not the whole story. It's just the first part of the verse. When you read the entire verse from Romans 6:23, it says, "For the wages of sin is death, but the gift of God is eternal life in Christ Jesus our Lord." There it is again, the forgiveness of our sin is clearly shown to be the gift of God.

In fact, there are dozens of verses in the Bible that say very clearly that salvation comes through placing our faith in Jesus Christ alone.

How can you receive this gift by placing your faith in Him?

The simplest and clearest answer is found just a few chapters later in the Bible, in Romans chapter 10. If you look in verses 9 and 10, you read this:

> If you declare with your mouth, "Jesus is Lord," and believe in your heart that God raised Him from the dead, you will be saved. For it is with your heart that you believe and are justified, and it is with your mouth that you profess your faith and are saved.

Those two verses tell you the "what" and the "why."

First, "declare with your mouth, 'Jesus is Lord,'" and believe in your heart that God raised Him from the dead. Just open your mouth and profess you faith. Talk to God and tell Him that you believe He raised Jesus from the dead so that He could offer you the gift of eternal life. Tell God you are declaring Jesus is your Lord.

---

[171] Romans 3:23
[172] Romans 6:23

It sounds so simple, right? And it is. Receiving a gift is always the simple part. When people want to give you a birthday gift, they have to decide what they want to give you, find the store carrying what they want to purchase, go to the store, buy the gift, wrap the gift, and then give it to you. That's much more complicated than your "job" as the recipient, right? All you have to do is receive the gift and say thank you.

Salvation is just the same. All you have to do is tell God you believe what He did through Jesus is sufficient and you want Him to be your Lord. That's it!

There are no special words needed. No special place to go or special position you need to be in. God doesn't care if you're sitting, standing, kneeling, or lying down. And if all you say is a simple prayer like, "God, I believe Jesus died and rose again to pay the price for my sins; and I want Him to be the Lord of my life" that is a profession of faith and God will answer your prayer.

You may be thinking that your sin is too big, and there is no way that God would ever forgive you. If so, you're not the first person who has felt that way. But, thankfully, there is another verse just a few verses later that speaks directly to that fear.

It says this: "Everyone who calls on the name of the Lord will be saved."[173]

Yeah—EVERYONE! No one is *too* bad, *too* sinful or *too* far away that God cannot reach him. If you want to place your faith in Jesus Christ, that's good enough for God.

And when you do, then you become part of the "IN CHRIST" group of people I've been talking about throughout this book. You become part of the family.

There are lots of wonderful churches that are part of this family. Some are sacramental, some evangelical, and some charismatic. There are some that focus on only one of those streams, others that focus on two or even all three of the streams. So, regardless of your preferred style of worshipping God, there will be a group of other believers that like that style, too.

The key thing is that you know you have a personal relationship with God. You *know* him, not just know *about* Him, because your relationship

[173] Romans 10:13

with Jesus is really just that—a relationship, not just a bunch of rules. I'll tell you, the more I've gotten to know Jesus, the more He has worked in my life and changed my character. It's tremendous!

ABOUT THE AUTHOR

Bishop Robert is a voice for unity in the Body of Christ. His heart's cry is the prayer of Jesus in John 17, that followers of Jesus may be one and so proclaim the message of the gospel in the power of His glory. He is a sought-after speaker who frequently travels internationally, sharing the message of unity in the Body of Christ. His ministry is characterized by an upraised index finger, demonstrating both the singular lordship of Jesus and Christ's command that His body be one.

Ordained to the ministry in 1999 in the Assemblies of God, Bishop Robert was consecrated as a bishop in the Communion of Evangelical Episcopal Churches (CEEC) on June 10, 2012, at the Garden Tomb in Jerusalem. The CEEC is a conservative communion of evangelical Christians who embrace all three historic streams of worship expressions in the church—the sacramental, the evangelical, and pentecostal.

Since being consecrated a bishop, he served as the assistant to the Presiding Bishop of the Communion of Evangelical Episcopal Churches, assisting in the global mission of the Communion. On account of his personal experience there in the time leading up to its becoming an independent nation, Bishop Robert was appointed as Bishop of South Sudan in January of 2013.

Because he has spent an average of six months a year for the past decade in Israel, Bishop Robert was also concurrently appointed as Bishop of the Mediterranean and Middle East, tasked with overseeing evangelism and church planting opportunities in that region.

Most recently, he was appointed as the Emissary for Christian Unitiy, assigning him to a global role working to advance the unity of the Body of Christ.

    Speaking requests can be made via email through his office, at *Info@BishopRobert.com*.

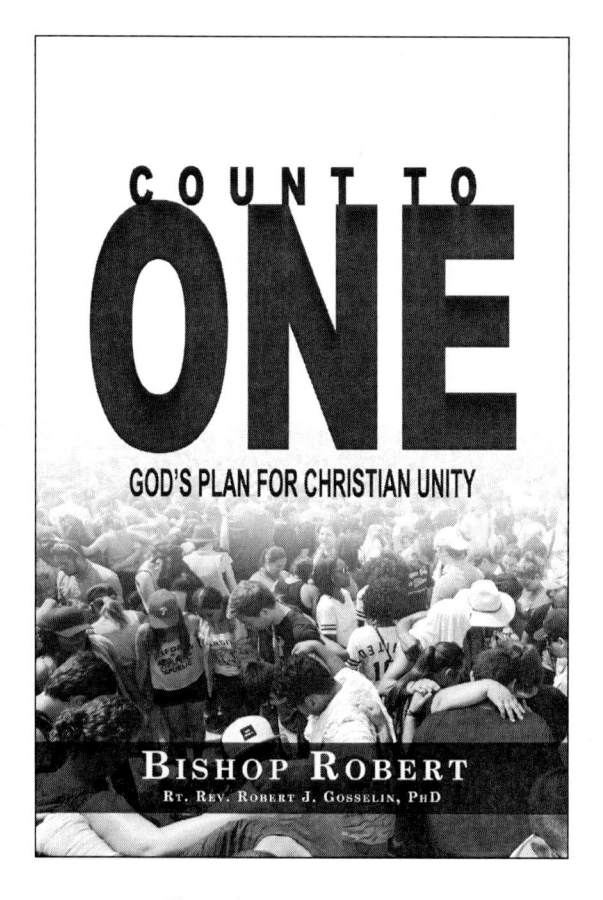

To order more copies of

COUNT TO ONE

contact Certa Publishing

- ❐ Order online at: CertaPublishing.com/CountToOne
- ❐ Call 855-77-CERTA or
- ❐ Email Info@CertaPublishing.com

Also available on Amazon.com